SOUTHERN
L I G H T
——COOKING——

SOUTHERN
L I G H T
——COOKING——

By Charles Pierce

A JOHN BOSWELL ASSOCIATES/KING HILL PRODUCTIONS BOOK

A PERIGEE BOOK

Perigee Books
are published by
The Putnam Publishing Group
200 Madison Avenue
New York, NY 10016

Library of Congress Cataloging-in-Publication Data

Pierce, Charles, date.
   Southern light cooking: easy, healthy, low-calorie recipes from BBQ to bourbon peach
shortcake / by Charles Pierce.
   p. cm.
   Includes index.
   ISBN 0-399-51808-8 (alk. paper)
   1. Cookery, American—Southern style.   I. Title.
TX715.2.S68P54   1993   92-21210 CIP
641.5975—dc20

Design by Nan Jernigan/The Colman Press
Cover illustration and design by Richard Rossiter
Printed in the United States of America

1 2 3 4 5 6 7 8 9 10

This book is printed on acid-free paper.
                    ∞

To Elizabeth Stewart, who taught me more about Southern cooking before I was six years old than many people learn in a lifetime.

To Wes Albinger and Trish Allen, the best taste testers around.

And to Mrs. Carolyn Nesmith, my Georgia friend who answered all my questions with accuracy and love.

CONTENTS

Bayou Seafood Gumbo, Buttermilk Corn Soup, Oyster Bisque and Turnip Green and Sausage Soup are just some of the spoon-it-up Southern goodness you'll find here.

Side salads, starter salads and fruit salads—such as Pear Salad with Blue Cheese and Bitter Greens, Grapefruit and Avocado Salad and Summer Stuffed Tomato Salad—are naturally light refreshers.

Whether oven-fried, stewed, roasted or grilled, these recipes are lean and tasty as can be. Jambalaya, Shady Tree Lemon Chicken, Chicken Breasts with Bourbon and Pecans and Tupelo Honey Cornish Hens are just a sampling of the new Southern way with poultry.

Calories and fat are still low and flavor is high in this chapter filled with down-home eating at its best. You'll be hard put to choose from recipes like Barbecued Beef, Ham with Red-Eye Gravy and Grits, Pork Chops Smothered in Tomatoes and Onions and Pork Medallions with Sherry and Pecans.

From farm-raised catfish to Gulf Coast oysters and ever-popular shrimp, seafood is simply a great way to eat light. Shrimp Creole, Baked Catfish with Red and Yellow Peppers, Deviled Crab and Lemon and Lime Baked Red Snapper are a sampling of the variety you'll find.

Puree of Sweet Potatoes and Apples with Ginger, Texas Cheese Grits, Creamed Corn with Tomatoes and Baked Stuffed Vidalia Onions are just some of the nutritious and delicious accompaniments that make a Southern meal so special.

Yes, there's Cornbread, Banana Bread, Buttermilk Biscuits and much more included here, with the light touch and controlled calories that allow baking without guilt.

Lightened versions of old-time classics and modern Southern sweets include Peach Bourbon Shortcakes, Key Lime Cheese Cakes, Blackberry Crumble, Meringue Plum Cake with Sherry and Kentucky Mint Ice.

Introduction

Southern cooking is an all-encompassing term. From the Chesapeake Bay to the Appalachian Mountains, across the flat, sea-bordered areas of South Carolina known as the Low Country, and on to the graceful foothills of northern Georgia, a fine tradition of good eating has developed over the last two centuries. From Florida, with its seafood and key limes, to the Mississippi Delta, and its spicy Cajun and Creole food, through Tennessee and Kentucky, with their barbecue and grits, there is an array of foods with a variety matched only by the topography of the land and the peoples who inhabit it.

Ethnic diversity has made a lasting mark on this part of the world. Native Americans taught early Southern settlers about raising corn and hunting and fishing in the New World. African-Americans introduced such staples as okra and yams, as well as a rich heritage of caring about good things from the earth. A decidedly French orientation in the kitchen comes not only from New Orleans plantation owners, but also from the many Huguenots who, fleeing religious persecution, settled in the Southern colonies in the late 1600s. Such influences created a melting pot of traditions that evolved into the unique cuisine that is known throughout the world as one of the finest expressions of great American cooking.

It is true that in the past Southern food was famous for its prodigious amounts of fatty salt pork, lard and sugar, with a heavy dose of flour thickening thrown in for good measure. That has changed, of course, as all of us, Southerners included, have become more aware of good nutrition and the many health benefits of eating lighter. While it was a challenge to adapt some of the classics, especially desserts and biscuits, to conform to restricted-calorie, low-fat and reduced-sodium guidelines, it was not as hard as you might think.

At its best, Southern food celebrates farm-fresh ingredients, with a bountiful array of colors and textures: ripe red tomatoes, orange sweet potatoes, green beans, sweet corn, onions, yellow squash, peas, collards and okra. Fish right off the line, peaches just in from the orchard and berries freshly picked from the bushes behind the house need only the lightest touch.

The goal of *Southern Light Cooking* is to capture the essence of this wonderful regional cuisine while providing a guide to lighter consumption. Portion sizes are important and so is choosing the leanest cuts. Meat, chicken and fish recipes call for three- to six-ounce well-trimmed servings, ample, according to today's guidelines, when served with plenty of vegetable and salad side dishes, as well as delightful regional specialties like grits and cornbread.

With careful thought, small amounts of bacon and ham have been added to select recipes for just that little bit of smoky flavor. In this way, Southern character is not compromised, and there is no excess gain in calories or cholesterol.

Sugar, also, has been used in smaller quantities than usual, with surprisingly good results, and egg whites often take the place of whole eggs. As a result, desserts are generous enough for an after-dinner treat without ignoring a sensible diet. By offering a relatively small portion and keeping sugar and fats to a minimum, the traditional Southern penchant for sweets is modified rather than eliminated.

Nothing prepares a food writer better for his or her career than a love of good eating. My father was the only boy of eleven children. He grew up in rural Alabama, across the river from Muscogee County, Georgia, where he met my mother, and I was raised. Eating well was a priority in our family, and I learned to appreciate tasty food at an early age. My father and my many aunts passed on to me a knowledge of and a passion for honest and oh, so satisfying, everyday Southern fare.

Since I grew up and left the South, I've studied classic French cuisine in Paris and spent most of my adult life in the land of the Yankees. But I always turn to my culinary roots for comfort and good home cooking. I hope modern cooks will find in this book a guide that provides an awareness of and great pleasure in the new, lighter and healthier Southern cooking.

About the Nutritional Numbers

All the recipes in *Southern Light Cooking* were developed with a reduced-calorie eating plan for an average healthy adult in mind. The maximum number of calories allowed were: 200 for first courses, whether appetizers, soups or starter salads; 400 for main courses; 175 for side, including vegetables, grains and breads; and 250 for desserts. Counts for many of the recipes in this book fall well below the maximum, which allows a great deal of freedom and diversity in menu planning.

Today's most up-to-date nutritional guidelines recommend that as a general rule no more than 30 percent of calories ingested come from fats. To help accomplish this goal, we've listed the percentage of calories from fat along with the calories per serving at the beginning of each recipe.

Many of the percentages here are low, but some do rise above 30 percent. Don't turn away; all these recipes contain very little fat. The perceptual problem comes when an exceptionally low-calorie dish contains even a little oil. For example, a lettuce salad with vinaigrette dressing made with a bare minimum of oil will have a high percentage of calories from fat because lettuce has exceptionally few calories and oil contains 40 per teaspoon. Also, since some foods, even nutritionally sound foods like fish, are naturally high in oils, it is impossible that every dish you eat meet this guideline. The important thing to remember is that 30 percent of all your calories from fat *over a two or three day period* should be no more than 30 percent. Just as with calorie counting, it is the total of all the foods you eat that is meaningful.

About the Ingredients

BOURBON—For two centuries, Southerners have enjoyed the rich flavor and aroma that bourbon whiskey brings to the kitchen. Made mostly in the South, this quintessentially American spirit takes its name from Bourbon County, Kentucky, the location of the earliest bourbon distilleries. Bourbon is made from a mixture of rye, barley and at least 51 percent corn. By law, it must be aged at least one year in new, charred-oak barrels, which add a vanilla scent to the sweet, fruity flavors that come from the grains. Bourbon mates perfectly with peaches, pecans and meats, making it the perfect liquor to deglaze a pan, to enrich a sauce or to add a delicious decadence to a dessert. Best of all, in cooking the alcohol and calories in bourbon go up in steam, leaving just the wonderful flavor and aroma behind.

CATFISH—These beady-eyed, bewhiskered creatures are not much to look at, but they make fine eating, as folks in the South have known for generations. Now in many areas outside the South, the catfish has practically replaced the flounder as the everyday "utility" fish. Fillets from grain-fed, farm-raised catfish are tender, light and delicately flavored, without the "fishiness" found in oilier species. And farm-raised catfish are even leaner than wild catfish. A 6-ounce farm-raised catfish fillet has only 150 calories, while offering more than 1 ounce of the highest quality protein.

CORNMEAL—With its pones, breads and puddings, the South has raised cornmeal from the role of mere staple to culinary stardom. Cornmeal comes in different varieties. The most common sort is produced at high speed by passing dried corn kernels between a series of steel rollers. Usually, these meals are also "degermed," meaning they're made from corn kernels from which the oily germ, the growing part of the seed, has been removed.

Stone-ground and water-ground cornmeal are whole-grain meals ground slowly between big old-fashioned millstones which, enthusiasts say, keeps the grain from getting too hot, which preserves more of its natural goodness. Stone-ground meals also have a smoother texture, which makes them better for cornmeal's typical uses in baked goods, for "breading" poultry and fish for frying and for cooking up as mush for breakfast.

By tradition, white cornmeal has been favored in the South, yellow cornmeal in the North. Yellow meal often has a slightly fuller, "cornier" flavor, but for recipe purposes the two are interchangeable.

GREENS—Turnip and mustard greens and collards traditionally were cooked with lard or fatback until they "melted in the mouth," an approach that destroyed most of the vitamins that greens offer and added unhealthy saturated fats and cholesterol. Today's approach emphasizes quick cooking and a minimum of added fat to make a "mess of greens" one of the healthiest, tastiest dishes you can put on your family's table. Greens are high in Vitamins A and C and low in calories.

Greens are available fresh or frozen, with fresh collards at peak season in midwinter and fresh mustard and turnip greens available year round. When using fresh greens, buy about 2½ pounds for a recipe that calls for 2 pounds of prepared greens. Be sure to choose the youngest, tenderest leaves available. Older, bigger leaves may be too bitter. Collards should be a clean frosty blue-green in color; mustard and turnip greens should be free from browning and bruising. Before using, wash greens in cold water, dipping and removing them several times and then draining them well. Remove any thick, tough stems.

Greens are very perishable and are best cooked and served the day of purchase. If they must be kept for a day or two, put them unwashed in plastic bags and place them in the coldest part of the refrigerator.

GRITS—Like potatoes, grits can turn up at Southern meals at any hour of the day—with fried eggs at breakfast, with red-eye gravy at lunch or served up in a casserole for dinner. What they are is ground hominy, which is dried corn with the hull and germ removed.

Grits come in "regular," "quick" and "instant" varieties. "Regular" and "quick" grits are identical except for granule size. The "quick" grits are smaller and cook faster. "Instant" grits are precooked and then dried again for packaging. They're "re-cooked" by the addition of boiling water. One problem with "instant" grits is that they're often highly salted in the original cooking. Because they've been freed of the oily germ, grits can be stored at room temperature and will keep for up to a year in a cool, dark place.

FATS AND OILS—For centuries, lard was the traditional cooking fat in the Southern kitchen, but it's rendered pork fat, which contains hefty amounts of cholesterol and other saturated fats that health authorities advise avoiding. Today's Southern cooks are moving away from heavy animal fats like lard and substituting vegetable products like the canola and safflower oils used in the recipes in this book. They are by far the healthier choice.

Admittedly, fats are roughly equal in caloric content—about 120 calories per tablespoon—but vegetable oils contain no cholesterol and little or no saturated fat, so they are much lighter and more healthful. Fats that are liquid at room temperature, such as safflower and canola oils, are lighter on the tongue than solid fats like lard.

Safflower oil is made from the seeds of a thistlelike plant native to the East Indies. It has a very high percentage of polyunsaturated fats and is often recommended to those on low-cholesterol diets. Safflower oil is delicate in texture, practically flavorless and has a very high smoke point.

Canola oil is a relative newcomer to American supermarkets, but has been around for years. It's made from the seeds of a plant with the unfortunate name of "rape." Some years ago, rapeseed growers up in Canada figured they'd never be able to retail their product without a name change, so they persuaded their government, and then ours, to let them call the stuff "canola," meaning "Canadian oil." It's good they did: canola oil is very low in saturated fats and very high in monounsaturates, which many health authorities believe help reduce low-density lipids in the blood, the so-called bad cholesterol. Canola is a bit more luxurious on the tongue than safflower oil and has a bit more flavor. It also has a high smoke point, which makes it good for frying.

MINT—Peppermint and spearmint are widely used in Southern cooking for their fresh, bright flavor. Spearmint, with light green leaves and stems, has the lighter, sweeter flavor; peppermint, with darker leaves and purplish stems, is the more pungent of the two. If you buy or pick more mint than you need, keep the leaves on the stems and put the stems in water, like flowers in a vase. The mint will keep fresh for weeks that way, often producing new roots.

Fresh mint is available at many supermarkets year round, and you can always try wintering over a mint plant or two in flowerpots placed near a sunny window. Many cooks like to freeze mint leaves for winter use. Lightly wash the leaves, pat them dry on paper towels, then put them in freezer bags. Dried mint leaves also have their use as a wintertime substitute for fresh mint. The flavor is not as fresh and bright, but it's better than no mint at all. Be sure to use only a third as much dried mint as fresh; for example, 1 teaspoon lightly crushed dried mint leaves for 1 tablespoon chopped fresh leaves.

OKRA—This traditional Southern vegetable is the fleshy seed pod of a plant related to the hollyhock. Okra flowers are a lovely butter yellow, and the green pods are long and tapered and slightly rough to the touch. Originally from West Africa, okra was cultivated by the natives there and brought by them to this country during the dark days of slavery. Folks in Louisiana call okra "gumbos," a word of Bantu origin, and gave the name "gumbo" to a whole family of soups and stews thickened with okra, which contains a kind of mucilage.

PECANS—These oblong, thin-shelled nuts come from a type of hickory tree native to the American South. Much prized in Southern cooking, the nuts are little known outside the United States. Pecans are available shelled or unshelled, with the latter sold in halves, pieces and chips. One pound of pecans in the shell will yield about 2¼ cups of nuts.

Shake a few nuts before buying unshelled pecans. If they rattle, the nuts are stale. Pecans coming to market have often spent many months in storage, but "new crop" pecans are available by mail order and offer the best flavor. In a tightly closed container, unshelled pecans will keep for two or three months at room temperature and up to six months in the refrigerator. Store shelled pecans in a sealed container for six months in the fridge and up to a year in the freezer.

If pecans will be used in a recipe without further cooking, they can be crisped and their flavor and aroma brightened by spreading the shelled nuts on a cookie sheet and baking them for about 7 minutes at 325° F.

SWEET POTATOES—Grown in the South as early as 1648, these are the thick, tuberous roots of a plant related to the morning glory, and so are the "yams" eaten by most Americans. Two kinds of sweet potatoes commonly show up in supermarkets: one has dry, mealy, pale-orange flesh; the flesh of the other kind is moist and deep yellow or reddish orange, and this "moist-flesh" kind is often misnamed a "yam." The two kinds can be hard to tell apart from their skins, so when shopping, it's always best to ask.

Sweet potatoes are usually available fresh year round; they're also commonly found in cans. (The sweet potato freezes only when it's fully cooked and is seldom freeze-packaged commercially.) When buying them fresh, look for sweet potatoes with smooth, clean skins, without shriveling or soft spots. Sweet potatoes are very perishable once deterioration begins, so it's usually best to buy no more than you intend to use within a week or so. Stored in perforated plastic bags, sweet potatoes will keep for a week to 10 days at room temperature. However, if you have an unheated spot in your house where the temperature stays between 45 and 50° F, you can often keep sweet potatoes for up to two months.

The true yam, rarely grown in the United States, is shaped like a sweet potato, but comes from a different family of plants and is usually much bigger, with some kinds growing to a weight of 100 pounds.

Chapter One

SOUPS
AND
GUMBOS

I have a feeling that good Southern soups come from the same kind of resourcefulness epitomized by Scarlet O'Hara in *Gone With the Wind*. Like good cooks everywhere, Southerners practice their own version of the art of frugal cooking. Rather than waste a couple of lone sweet potatoes, they toss them into a pot, add some aromatic vegetables, broth and seasoning, and suddenly it's soup. This making do must be part of what makes soups feel so good for the soul.

Having grown up in the warmth of the South, I favor light soups with clean, flavorful bases. Red, ripe tomatoes, fresh beans, peas, okra, squash, corn and greens are all wonderful soup vegetables that are low in calories, colorful and full of healthful vitamins and minerals. Combined with good broth, or even just water, a few herbs and some special seasonings, these soups can provide the perfect beginning to a meal.

On the other end of the spectrum are those distinctly Southern, thick and chunky, concoctions, often mixing in chicken, sausage, seafood or both, that bridge the gap between soup and stew. Recipes for gumbos and for Brunswick Stew, which is served as an accompaniment to barbecue, but could just as easily be a meal in itself, fall into this category.

The best base for any good soup is homemade stock, and I've included recipes for a chicken stock and a simple fish stock. But because we often don't have the time for that extra step, most of the recipes in this chapter were tested with reduced-sodium canned chicken broth, available in supermarkets all over the country.

As a meal starter or as the main event, nothing is quite as satisfying as what you can spoon up with a big spoon. Most of these soups can be made in advance and heated up at the last minute. And to dress up any of them, all you need are a handful of chopped fresh herbs, a tiny dice of colorful vegetables, a dollop of plain low-fat yogurt or a pinch of finely chopped nuts.

Cold Yellow Pepper Soup

4 Servings   64% Calories from fat   128 Calories per serving

2 large yellow bell peppers, quartered
2 tablespoons extra-virgin olive oil
2 shallots, minced
⅛ teaspoon crushed hot red pepper
1 cup dry white wine
4 cups reduced-sodium canned chicken broth
Pinch of saffron threads
¼ teaspoon salt
¼ teaspoon freshly ground pepper
2 ounces lean ham, thinly shredded (½ cup)
6 black olives, pitted and halved
4 to 6 large basil leaves, shredded

1. In a large saucepan, bring 3 cups water to a boil over high heat. Add the peppers and cook about 3 minutes to loosen the skins. Drain under cold running water and peel off skins. Cut 2 of the pepper quarters into tiny dice and set aside for garnish.

2. In a large saucepan, heat the olive oil over medium-high heat. Add the remaining peppers, the shallots and the hot pepper. Cook, stirring, until the shallots are slightly softened, 1 to 2 minutes. Pour in the white wine and the chicken broth. Increase the heat to high and bring to a boil. Add the saffron and boil, stirring occasionally, until reduced by one-third, about 20 minutes.

3. Transfer the soup to a food processor and puree until smooth. Season with the salt and pepper. Let cool to room temperature, cover and refrigerate until well chilled, 2 hours or overnight.

4. Just before serving, divide the soup among 4 chilled individual bowls. Garnish with the reserved diced yellow pepper, the ham, olives and shredded basil leaves.

South Carolina Chicken and Rice Soup

6 TO 8 SERVINGS   26% CALORIES FROM FAT   367 CALORIES PER SERVING

2 tablespoons butter
1 medium onion, finely chopped
1 celery rib, thinly sliced
3 tablespoons flour
4 cups homemade Chicken Stock (recipe follows) or reduced-sodium
   canned broth
1 chicken, 3½ pounds, cut into 6 or 8 pieces, skin and fat removed
½ cup rice
½ teaspoon salt
2 medium carrots, peeled and cut into ½-inch dice
1 cup frozen green peas
¼ teaspoon freshly ground pepper
1 tablespoon chopped fresh thyme leaves or 1 teaspoon dried

1. In a large saucepan or soup kettle, melt the butter over medium-high heat. Add the onion and celery and cook, stirring frequently, until softened, about 3 minutes. Add the flour and cook, stirring, for 1 minute. Whisk in the chicken stock, raise the heat to high and bring to a boil. Cook, stirring frequently, until slightly thickened, about 5 minutes.

2. Place the chicken in the pot, reduce the heat to medium-low and simmer, partially covered, until tender, 45 minutes to 1 hour.

3. Meanwhile, bring 1 cup water to a boil in a small saucepan. Add the rice and ¼ teaspoon of the salt and return to a boil. Reduce the heat to medium-low, cover and cook 20 minutes.

4. Transfer the chicken to a plate or platter to cool. Skim off all fat from the surface of the soup. Add the carrots and rice to the soup and cook over medium heat until the carrots are tender, 7 to 10 minutes.

5. When the chicken is cool enough to handle, pull the meat from the bones and remove all skin, fat and gristle. Cut the chicken into large chunks. Return the chicken to the soup and add the peas, pepper, thyme and remaining ¼ teaspoon salt. Simmer over medium heat until the peas are tender and the soup is heated through, about 5 minutes. Serve hot.

Chicken Stock

Makes about 1½ quarts

5 pounds chicken parts (backs, necks, feet, wings or thighs)
3 medium onions, peeled and quartered
3 carrots, peeled and cut into 1-inch pieces
2 celery ribs, cut into 1-inch pieces
1 bay leaf, crumpled
1 teaspoon peppercorns
½ teaspoon salt

1. Trim the chicken parts of all fat. Place the chicken in a stockpot with the onions, carrots, celery, bay leaf and peppercorns. Pour in 3 quarts of water and add the salt.

2. Bring the stock to a boil, skimming off any foam that comes to the top. Reduce the heat to low and simmer gently for at least 2 hours. Add additional cold water frequently, about ½ cup at a time, and let return to a simmer. This will force impurities to rise to the surface so that they can easily be skimmed off, resulting in a clear, rich stock.

3. Strain the stock, discarding the bones and vegetables. Let cool to room temperature, cover and refrigerate overnight. The next day, remove the congealed fat from the surface.

Brunswick Stew

Brunswick stew is as popular in the South as R.C. Cola and Moon Pies. This is not a delicate soup. Families would throw anything they had into the pot, and some original versions include pig's head, pig's feet, liver, squirrel and sometimes possum. Don't worry, this lighter—and more modern— recipe just uses chicken.

8 SERVINGS   16% CALORIES FROM FAT   204 CALORIES PER SERVING

1 whole chicken, 3½ pounds, trimmed of fat
2 cups fresh or frozen corn kernels
1 can (28 ounces) whole peeled tomatoes, drained and coarsely chopped
2 cups sliced okra or green beans
1 cup canned and drained or thawed frozen lima beans
2 medium onions, thinly sliced
½ teaspoon salt
¼ teaspoon freshly ground pepper

1. Place the chicken in a large soup kettle and add enough cold water to cover by 2 inches. Bring to a boil over medium-high heat, reduce the heat to medium-low and simmer 1½ to 2 hours, skimming occasionally. Remove the chicken to a bowl and set aside to cool. Reserve the broth in the kettle.

2. When the chicken is cool enough to handle, pull the meat from the bones, discarding all the skin, bones and gristle. Cut the chicken into large cubes. Skim off all the fat from the top of the broth in the kettle.

3. Return the chicken to the pot. Add the corn, tomatoes, okra, lima beans and onions. Season with the salt and pepper. Bring to a boil, reduce the heat to medium and simmer uncovered, stirring often, until slightly thickened, 30 to 40 minutes.

Buttermilk Corn Soup

With only 1½ percent fat, buttermilk is a light ingredient, which belies its rich name. Actually, it contributes a lovely nutty creaminess with relatively few calories.

6 SERVINGS   15% CALORIES FROM FAT   105 CALORIES PER SERVING

> *1 small onion, finely chopped*
> *3 cups fresh or frozen corn kernels*
> *1 tablespoon flour*
> *1½ cups buttermilk*
> *1½ cups reduced-sodium canned chicken broth*
> *½ teaspoon salt*
> *¼ teaspoon freshly ground pepper*
> *1 tablespoon chopped parsley*

1. Coat the bottom of a large saucepan with vegetable cooking spray. Add the onion and cook over medium heat, stirring constantly, until softened, about 2 minutes. Add the corn and stir in the flour to coat. Pour in the buttermilk and broth. Raise the heat to medium-high and bring to a boil, stirring frequently. Reduce the heat to medium-low and simmer, stirring occasionally, about 10 minutes.

2. Transfer the soup to a food processor and pulse several times until coarsely pureed, about 10 seconds. Return the soup to the saucepan and season with the salt and pepper. Gently reheat over low heat. Stir in the parsley just before serving.

She-Crab Soup

This is an old Charleston favorite. The original name lingers, though generic crabmeat is called for here, rather than almost impossible-to-find "she-crab." Females are supposed to be a bit tastier than he-crabs, or so it goes. More important, the delicate eggs of the female are a traditional ingredient added mostly for texture. I've lightened up the recipe that follows by using less fat and fewer calories while retaining the flavor that makes the soup so special. Crabmeat is probably a lot more expensive along the streets of Charleston (where vendors used to make a point of selling she-crabs for more money than the lowly he-crabs) today than it used to be. Substitute surimi or finely chopped shrimp to make the soup less costly.

6 SERVINGS   29% CALORIES FROM FAT   178 CALORIES PER SERVING

2 tablespoons butter
1 tablespoon minced onion
1 tablespoon flour
4 cups skim milk
¼ teaspoon salt
¼ teaspoon freshly ground pepper
⅛ teaspoon grated nutmeg
2 cups lump crabmeat
2 hard-cooked egg whites, finely chopped
4 to 6 tablespoons dry sherry
Paprika

1. In a large saucepan, melt the butter over medium-high heat. Add the onion and cook, stirring often, until softened, about 2 minutes. Add the flour and cook, stirring, for 1 minute. Slowly whisk in the milk. Bring to a boil, stirring, until slightly thickened, 1 to 2 minutes. Reduce heat to low.

2. Season with the salt, pepper and nutmeg. Add the crab and egg whites and simmer, stirring often, 15 minutes.

3. Just before serving, place about 1 tablespoon sherry in the bottom of each soup bowl. Add the soup and dust the top with paprika. Serve at once.

Oyster Bisque

Oysters are plentiful all along the Gulf Coast, and Southerners eat them raw, scalloped, fried, in chunky gumbos and in creamy soups, such as this one. Naturally rich in protein and minerals and very low in calories, the shellfish are perfect for gussying up just a bit. The French influence on some parts of Southern cooking is evident in this lovely, light soup, elegant enough to start your best dinner party. Note: The "liquor" is the oyster liquid. Be sure to ask your fishmonger to save it for you.

6 SERVINGS   35% CALORIES FROM FAT   161 CALORIES PER SERVING

> 2 celery ribs, thinly sliced
> 2 tablespoons butter
> 2 tablespoons flour
> 4 cups skim milk
> 1 pint shucked oysters, with their liquor reserved
> 1/2 teaspoon salt
> 1/4 teaspoon freshly ground pepper
> Paprika

1. In a small saucepan, bring 2 cups water to a boil over high heat. Add the celery, reduce the heat to medium-low and simmer until softened, 5 to 7 minutes. Let cool slightly, then transfer to a food processor and puree until smooth.

2. In a medium saucepan, melt the butter over medium heat. Add the flour and cook, stirring, 1 minute. Whisk in the milk and bring to a boil, whisking often until smooth and thickened, 2 to 3 minutes. Stir in the celery puree, reduce the heat to low and simmer, stirring occasionally, 3 minutes.

3. Place the oysters with their liquor in a small saucepan. Cook over low heat until the oysters are plumped and their edges curl, about 5 minutes. Drain the oysters, reserving the liquid. Coarsely chop the oysters.

4. Add the chopped oysters and reserved liquid to the celery base. Bring to a simmer over medium-low heat. Season the soup with the salt and pepper. Serve in individual bowls, garnished with a dusting of paprika.

Great Gumbo

The traditional gumbo was thickened with filé gumbo powder made from finely ground sassafras root or with okra. For health reasons, filé powder is no longer recommended, so I've thickened this gumbo with okra and a small amount of flour. Calories permitting, serve gumbo in individual bowls containing about ½ cup steamed white rice.

6 SERVINGS   34% CALORIES FROM FAT   182 CALORIES PER SERVING

1 tablespoon canola or safflower oil
1 medium onion, finely chopped
1 green bell pepper, finely chopped
2 celery ribs, thinly sliced
2 tablespoons flour
3 medium tomatoes, peeled, seeded and chopped, or 1 small can (16 ounces) whole tomatoes, drained and chopped
1 package (10 ounces) frozen sliced okra
2 cans (14¾ ounces each) reduced-sodium chicken broth
½ teaspoon dried oregano
½ teaspoon salt
¼ teaspoon pepper
¼ teaspoon cayenne pepper
Vegetable cooking spray
1 large chicken breast, about 6 ounces, cut into 1-inch cubes
½ pound spicy Italian turkey sausage, cut into ½-inch slices
¼ pound medium shrimp, shelled, deveined and cut into 1-inch pieces

1. In a large nonstick saucepan or Dutch oven, heat the oil over medium-high heat. Add the onion, pepper and celery. Cook, stirring often, until slightly softened, about 5 minutes. Sprinkle the flour over the vegetables and cook, stirring often, 2 minutes longer. Stir in the tomatoes, okra and broth. Season with the oregano, salt, pepper and cayenne. Partially cover and cook over medium-low heat, stirring occasionally, until thickened, 45 minutes to 1 hour.

2. Coat a large nonstick skillet with vegetable cooking spray. Add the chicken, sausage and shrimp. Cook over medium-high heat, tossing and stirring constantly, until the shrimp have turned bright pink and the chicken and sausage are lightly browned, about 3 minutes.

3. Ladle in about ½ cup of the gumbo and bring to a boil, stirring constantly. Stir this mixture into the large pan of gumbo and simmer 5 minutes longer, until the meats are completely cooked through and the flavors have developed.

Georgia Gumbo

Here is a light, all-vegetable gumbo made with the basics: onion, tomatoes and okra, the African name for which gave *gumbo* its name. Serve this soup with rice or a green vegetable and corn muffins.

4 SERVINGS   35% CALORIES FROM FAT   102 CALORIES PER SERVING

> *1 tablespoon safflower or canola oil*
> *1 medium onion, thinly sliced*
> *1 can (28 ounces) Italian peeled tomatoes, drained and coarsely chopped*
> *2 cups sliced okra*
> *2 cups reduced-sodium canned chicken broth or water*
> *½ teaspoon salt*
> *¼ teaspoon freshly ground pepper*

1. In a large nonstick skillet, heat the oil over medium-high heat. Add the onion and cook, stirring occasionally, until softened, about 3 minutes.

2. Stir in the tomatoes, okra and broth. Season with the salt and pepper and cook, partially covered, stirring often, until thick enough to be eaten with a fork, about 1 hour.

Bayou Seafood Gumbo

This is one of those Southern coastal dishes that can be varied according to what seafood is freshest in your market at the moment. I've used shrimp and oysters. Crabmeat, which is common in the South but quite expensive in the north, has a rich, sweet flavor; it can take the place of the shrimp. Scallops can be added, as can any lean, white-fleshed fish, such as snapper, flounder or even catfish.

To lighten this classic Creole dish, I've omitted the *roux,* a flour and fat thickener. I've also kept the gumbo meatless. With all the flavors going on here, you won't miss a thing. As light as it is, this is one of those hearty soups that can easily double as a main-course stew.

6 SERVINGS   27% CALORIES FROM FAT   279 CALORIES PER SERVING

> 2 tablespoons canola or safflower oil
> 1 medium onion, finely chopped
> 1 celery rib, finely chopped
> 1 garlic clove, minced
> ½ cup long-grain white rice
> 3 or 4 large tomatoes, peeled, seeded and chopped, or 1 can (28 ounces) whole peeled tomatoes, drained and chopped
> 1 pound fresh okra, sliced, or 1 package (14 ounces) sliced frozen okra
> 2 cups Simple Fish Stock (recipe follows) or 1 cup bottled clam juice diluted with 1 cup water or 2 cups water
> 1 bay leaf
> 1 tablespoon chopped parsley
> ½ teaspoon salt
> ½ teaspoon freshly ground black pepper
> ⅛ teaspoon cayenne pepper, or more to taste
> 1 pound medium shrimp, shelled and deveined
> 1 pint shucked oysters

1. In a large nonreactive saucepan or flameproof casserole, heat the oil over medium-high heat. Add the onion, celery and garlic. Cook, stirring often, until softened, about 3 minutes.

2. Stir in the rice and cook, stirring, until the grains are glossy, about 1 minute. Add the tomatoes, okra, fish stock, bay leaf, parsley, salt, black pepper and cayenne. Raise the heat to high and bring to a boil. Reduce the heat to medium-low and simmer, stirring often, until thickened, about 1 hour.

3. While the soup is simmering, cut the shrimp into ½-inch dice. When the gumbo is thickened, add the shrimp and oysters to the soup, reduce the heat to medium and simmer for 10 minutes. Serve hot.

Simple Fish Stock

For best results, use the bones and scraps of lean white fish like sole, flounder, whiting or sea bass. Rinse the bones under cold running water before making the stock. Do not cook for more than 20 minutes, as fish bones can turn bitter if overcooked.

MAKES ABOUT 1 QUART

1 tablespoon vegetable oil
1 medium onion, finely chopped
1½ to 2 pounds fish bones and scraps, cut into 2-inch pieces
½ teaspoon salt
¼ teaspoon freshly ground pepper

1. In a large saucepan or soup kettle, heat the oil over medium-high heat. Add the onion and cook, stirring frequently, until softened, about 3 minutes. Add the fish bones and cook, stirring, 2 minutes longer.

2. Pour in 4 cups water and season with the salt and pepper. Raise the heat to high and bring to a boil. Reduce the heat to medium and simmer, partially covered, for 20 minutes. Strain and let cool to room temperature if not using immediately. Cover and refrigerate for up to 3 days, until ready to use or freeze for up to 1 month.

Sweet Potato Soup

At only 115 calories per medium potato, sweet potatoes are a diet-conscious diner's treat, rich as well in Vitamin A and niacin. Here the bright, citrusy flavor of fresh orange juice enlivens the natural sweetness of the potatoes.

6 SERVINGS   10% CALORIES FROM FAT   146 CALORIES PER SERVING

> *3 medium sweet potatoes (about 2 pounds), peeled and cut into 1-inch chunks*
> *3 cups reduced-sodium canned chicken broth*
> *½ cup fresh orange juice*
> *2 teaspoons Dijon mustard*
> *¼ teaspoon salt*
> *¼ teaspoon freshly ground pepper*
> *Dash of cayenne pepper*
> *6 teaspoons reduced-calorie sour cream*
> *1½ teaspoons minced orange zest*

1. Place the sweet potato chunks in a large saucepan and add the chicken broth. Bring to a boil, reduce the heat to medium and cook, partially covered, stirring occasionally, until the sweet potatoes are tender, about 20 minutes.

2. Working in batches, if necessary, puree the soup in a blender or food processor until very smooth. Return to the saucepan and bring to a simmer over low heat. Stir in the orange juice, mustard, salt, pepper and cayenne. Serve at once in individual bowls, garnished with 1 teaspoon of sour cream and ¼ teaspoon minced orange zest.

Turnip Green and Sausage Soup

In the South, we like to use all parts of the vegetables, especially the nutritious green tops. Greens and meat broth, usually from some part of the pig, are a common pairing. These days we are lucky to have lean, low-fat sausages made from the much lighter meat of turkey and chicken to use in place of pork. (Note: If turnip greens are not available, the soup can be made with spinach or Swiss chard.)

4 SERVINGS   50% CALORIES FROM FAT   163 CALORIES PER SERVING

> *1 pound baby turnip greens*
> *1 tablespoon canola or safflower oil*
> *1 medium onion, thinly sliced*
> *2 cans (14½ ounces each) reduced-sodium chicken broth*
> *½ pound turkey Polish kielbasa sausage, cut into ¼-inch-thick slices*
> *¼ teaspoon salt*
> *¼ teaspoon freshly ground pepper*

1. Remove the large stems from the turnip greens. Rinse the leaves well. With a large stainless steel knife, thinly shred or chop the greens.

2. In a large saucepan, heat the oil over medium-high heat. Add the onion and cook, stirring often, until softened, about 3 minutes.

3. Add the turnip greens to the pan and stir to blend with the onions. Pour in the broth; add the sausage, salt and pepper. Bring to a boil, reduce the heat to medium-low and simmer until the greens are cooked and the sausage is heated through, 10 to 15 minutes.

— Southern-Style Vegetable Soup with Squash, Okra and Peppers

6 Servings   41% Calories from fat   149 Calories per serving

2 celery ribs, finely chopped
3 medium carrots, halved lengthwise and thinly sliced
1 medium onion, finely chopped
½ green bell pepper, finely chopped
½ red bell pepper, finely chopped
2 tablespoons safflower or canola oil
½ small head of green cabbage, finely shredded
2 medium tomatoes, peeled, seeded and chopped
6 cups reduced-sodium canned chicken broth
½ teaspoon salt
¼ teaspoon freshly ground pepper
1 medium yellow squash, halved lengthwise and cut into 1-inch pieces
1 medium zucchini, halved lengthwise and cut into 1-inch pieces
5 okra, cut into ½-inch pieces

1. In a large saucepan or soup kettle, combine the celery, carrots, onion, green pepper, red pepper and oil. Cook over medium-high heat, stirring occasionally, until softened, about 5 minutes. Add the cabbage and tomatoes and cook until the cabbage wilts and the tomatoes begin to give off liquid, about 3 minutes.

2. Pour in the chicken broth, season with the salt and pepper and simmer 10 minutes. Add the yellow squash, zucchini and okra and cook until tender, 8 to 10 minutes longer.

Yellow Squash Soup with Lemon

4 SERVINGS   19% CALORIES FROM FAT   64 CALORIES PER SERVING

6 small yellow squash (about 1½ pounds total), trimmed and cut into
   1-inch pieces
1 medium onion, thinly sliced
4 cups reduced-sodium canned chicken broth or water
¼ teaspoon salt
¼ teaspoon freshly ground pepper
½ small lemon

1. In a large saucepan, combine the squash and onion. Add the chicken broth and season with the salt and pepper.

2. Trim off the ends of the lemon half down to the pulp and cut the lemon into paper-thin slices. Add to the pot and bring to a simmer over medium-high heat. Cook, stirring occasionally, until the squash and onions are tender and the lemon is translucent, 10 to 15 minutes.

3. Working in batches, if necessary, puree the soup in a blender or food processor until smooth. Return to the saucepan and bring to a simmer over medium-low heat. Season with additional salt and pepper to taste and serve hot.

Chilled Tomato and Cucumber Soup with Fresh Basil

Tomatoes and cucumbers—both exceptionally light, versatile vegetables—grow like weeds in the South, so we are always looking for new ways to use them. This is a cool, uncooked soup, perfect for the hottest part of summer, which can be enjoyed on the veranda or patio as well as at the table.

6 SERVINGS   16% CALORIES FROM FAT   94 CALORIES PER SERVING

4 large, ripe tomatoes (2 pounds)
2 cups loosely packed basil leaves
1 medium cucumber, peeled, seeded and thickly sliced
2 cups low-fat plain yogurt
1 teaspoon fresh lemon juice
¼ teaspoon salt
¼ teaspoon freshly ground black pepper
Dash of cayenne pepper

1. Bring a large saucepan of water to a boil. Drop in the tomatoes and boil 30 to 60 seconds, until the skins begin to loosen slightly. Drain into a colander and rinse under cold running water to cool. Cut out the cores and slip the skins off the tomatoes by pulling them between your thumb and a small knife. Cut the tomatoes in half and gently squeeze out the seeds. Coarsely chop the tomatoes.

2. Rinse and drain the basil. Remove about 18 of the smallest leaves and set them aside for garnish. Place the remaining basil in a food processor.

3. Add the tomatoes and cucumbers to the basil and puree until smooth. Pour into a large bowl and whisk in the yogurt until blended. Season with the lemon juice, salt, black pepper and cayenne. Cover and refrigerate until well chilled, at least 2 hours or overnight.

4. Just before serving, ladle the soup into chilled bowls. Garnish with the reserved basil leaves.

Chapter Two

SALADS

In the lush, warm climate of the South, which fosters the growth of so many fresh greens, cool, crisp salads have always been popular. There is nothing quite like the crunch of coleslaw made with thinly shredded, just-picked cabbage tossed with a sprightly tart dressing. It is the perfect combination with barbecue. And there are so many variations on every theme.

Typically Southern salad ingredients are easy to come by. Fresh lettuce, celery, carrots, tomatoes, even tender greens, such as collards or turnip greens, are full of flavor and nutrition, not to speak of fiber, and low in calories. Okra, avocados and dandelion greens, which we pick ourselves, are about as exotic as it gets.

When it comes to dressings, you'll notice I've strayed from tradition. The South has long been notorious for its use of bacon fat, sugar and flour, even in salad. Here I've kept the spirit of the place but taken off quite a "weight." Canola and safflower oils have been chosen for their light flavor and low percentage of saturated fat. Low-fat yogurt mixed with fresh herbs and a touch of vinegar makes an excellent creamy dressing. Low-fat cottage cheese blended until smooth in a food processor and mixed with a tablespoon of reduced-calorie mayonnaise is another good trick. Chicken broth and fresh citrus juice takes the place of part of some of the oil in many of the recipes that follow. Of course, in a pinch, there are many good-quality, reduced-calorie bottled brands out there, ready to shake and pour.

Fruit salads, also included here, can be savory or sweet. Pear Salad with Blue Cheese and Bitter Greens makes a striking first course, while

Fresh Fruit Salad with Honey and Lemon is best served as a refresher at the end of the meal.

Whether you choose to use it as a first course, side dish or light lunch, salad can be an important part of any meal. Use the freshest ingredients you can find and treat them with respect, following the Southern tradition I learned for good eating in all categories.

Green Apple Salad with Hickory Nuts

Southern green apples are small and tart. Granny Smith apples will do if these aren't available, but use only two because they are larger. Hickory nuts are a down-home treat. Thick hulled and wild, rather than cultivated, these intensely flavored nuts have a distinctive taste that marries well with apples. Use walnuts if hickory nuts are not obtainable.

4 SERVINGS   43% CALORIES FROM FAT   183 CALORIES PER SERVING

> 3 tart green apples, peeled and cut into ½-inch dice
> 1 tablespoon fresh lemon juice
> ¼ cup coarsely chopped hickory nuts or walnuts
> ¼ cup reduced-calorie mayonnaise
> ½ cup nonfat plain yogurt
> 2 celery ribs, peeled and thinly sliced
> 4 Boston or romaine lettuce leaves

1. Preheat the oven to 350° F. In a small bowl, toss the diced apples with the lemon juice to prevent discoloration and set aside. Arrange the hickory nuts over the bottom of a small baking dish. Place in the oven and toast, stirring occasionally, until lightly browned, about 5 minutes. Let cool completely.

2. In a medium bowl, stir the mayonnaise with the yogurt until well blended. Add the apples, celery and hickory nuts, stir to coat, cover and refrigerate for 1 hour.

3. Place 1 lettuce leaf on each of 4 plates. Top each with one-fourth of the apple salad.

Beet and Watercress Salad with Pecans

All root vegetables are popular in the South, and beets are no exception. Watercress is actually a wild green, which can be found along the banks of many streams in the countryside. The sweetness of the beets and pecans in contrast to the sharpness of the watercress creates a salad that is delicious as well as beautiful, and substantial enough to serve as a first course. To keep calories and fat light, orange juice has been substituted for half of the oil in the dressing.

4 SERVINGS   59% CALORIES FROM FAT   125 CALORIES PER SERVING

> 1 pound beets (5 small or 4 medium) or 1 can (16 ounces) whole baby beets
> 1 teaspoon Dijon mustard
> 1/4 teaspoon salt
> 1/8 teaspoon freshly ground pepper
> 2 tablespoons red wine vinegar
> 2 tablespoons canola or safflower oil
> 2 tablespoons orange juice
> 1 small onion, halved lengthwise and thinly sliced
> 1 large bunch of watercress, tough stems removed
> 1 1/2 tablespoons chopped pecans

1. If using fresh beets, trim off the tops, leaving about 3 inches of the green. In a large saucepan of boiling water, cook the beets 30 to 40 minutes, or until tender to the center when pierced with a small knife. Drain into a colander and rinse under cold water until cool enough to handle. Trim the tops and roots off the beets and peel off the skins. If using canned beets, drain them. Cut the beets into 1/2-inch dice.

2. In a medium bowl, whisk together the mustard, salt, pepper and vinegar. Gradually whisk in the oil and orange juice until well blended. Add the beets and sliced onion and stir gently until well coated with the dressing. Cover and refrigerate for at least 2 hours, or until chilled.

3. To serve, make a bed of watercress on each of 4 salad plates. Spoon the beets and onion on top, dividing evenly. Garnish with the pecans.

Collard Green Salad with Mushrooms and Orange-Lemon Vinaigrette

Young tender greens are an important part of this salad. Older, tougher greens need to be blanched first in boiling salted water.

6 Servings   47% Calories from fat   87 Calories per serving

1 tablespoon fresh lemon juice
1 teaspoon Dijon mustard
¼ teaspoon salt
¼ teaspoon freshly ground pepper
2 tablespoons vegetable oil
2 tablespoons orange juice
1½ pounds baby collard greens, trimmed, with tough stems removed
6 ounces medium mushrooms, thinly sliced

1. In a medium bowl, whisk together the lemon juice, mustard, salt and pepper. Slowly drizzle in the oil and the orange juice, whisking continuously until emulsified. Set the orange-lemon vinaigrette aside.

2. Place several collard leaves on top of each other and cut, a few at a time, into thin strips. Place the shredded leaves in a large bowl. Add the mushrooms, pour on the orange-lemon vinaigerette and toss and stir to combine.

Coleslaw

4 SERVINGS   24% CALORIES FROM FAT   60 CALORIES PER SERVING

2 medium carrots, peeled and grated
½ pound green cabbage, thinly shredded
½ cup low-fat plain yogurt
1 tablespoon reduced-calorie mayonnaise
1 teaspoon Dijon mustard
1 tablespoon fresh lemon juice
¼ teaspoon freshly ground pepper

1. In a large bowl, toss the carrots with the cabbage. In a small bowl, combine the yogurt, mayonnaise, mustard, lemon juice and pepper. Stir well to blend.

2. Pour the dressing over the carrots and cabbage. Toss well to coat. Cover and refrigerate until chilled, about 1 hour.

Spring Dandelion Salad

Frugal Southerners have long cherished the tender dandelion leaves that appear in the early part of spring. Tougher, older dandelion greens should be cooked and are therefore not suitable for salad.

4 SERVINGS   44% CALORIES FROM FAT   95 CALORIES PER SERVING

½ pound fresh dandelion greens, stems removed
3 ounces lean ham, cut into thin slivers
1 tablespoon canola or safflower oil
1 garlic clove, crushed through a press
3 tablespoons red wine vinegar

2 hard-cooked egg whites, finely chopped
½ teaspoon salt
¼ teaspoon freshly ground pepper

1. Arrange the dandelion in a large serving bowl. Sprinkle the slivers of ham over the greens. In a small bowl, combine the oil, garlic and vinegar. Beat with a fork to blend.

2. Just before serving, pour the dressing over the salad. Sprinkle on the chopped egg whites and season with the salt and pepper. Toss well and serve at once.

— *Fresh Fruit Salad with Honey and Lemon* —

4 SERVINGS   2% CALORIES FROM FAT   132 CALORIES PER SERVING

¼ cup honey
2 tablespoons fresh lemon juice
2 ripe peaches, peeled and sliced
2 plums, pitted and sliced
1 cup fresh blackberries
2 tablespoons chopped fresh mint
Several whole mint leaves, for garnish

1. In a small bowl, mix the honey with the lemon juice, stirring until dissolved. Cover and refrigerate for at least 1 hour.

2. In a medium bowl, combine the peaches, plums and blackberries. Pour the chilled honey mixture over the fruit and stir to blend. Sprinkle with the chopped mint just before serving and mound in chilled bowls. Garnish with the mint leaves.

Grapefruit and Avocado Salad

Avocados are sometimes called alligator pears in Southern cooking. White or pink grapefruit can be used here, but the pink makes for a prettier salad.

4 SERVINGS   63% CALORIES FROM FAT   166 CALORIES PER SERVING

> *1 medium avocado, peeled, halved lengthwise and pitted*
> *1 tablespoon fresh lemon juice*
> *2 grapefruits*
> *1 teaspoon Dijon mustard*
> *½ teaspoon salt*
> *⅛ teaspoon freshly ground pepper*
> *2 tablespoons red wine vinegar*
> *4 teaspoons canola or safflower oil*
> *2 tablespoons orange juice*

1. Cut the avocado halves lengthwise into 8 wedges and sprinkle with the lemon juice to prevent discoloration. Peel the grapefruits, removing all the bitter white pith and cut between the membranes to remove whole sections. Alternate avocado and grapefruit pieces on 4 individual serving plates.

2. In a small bowl, combine the mustard, salt and pepper. Whisk in the vinegar. Slowly whisk in the oil and orange juice and beat until well blended. Spoon equal amounts of the dressing over the salads and serve at once.

Okra Salad

The inspiration for this recipe comes from an old Southern cookbook called *Mrs. Dull's Southern Cooking*. Mrs. Dull was the food editor of the *Atlanta Journal* for years in the early part of this century. Her book, published in 1928, served as the bible for many young Southern ladies. Long out of print, the book is still a part of many family libraries and is often referred to even today.

Okra is more versatile than you might think. It is important to use small, young pods for this salad. The older ones are tougher and don't look as nice on the plate. Strips of roasted red pepper or pimiento can be added for color if you like.

4 SERVINGS   69% CALORIES FROM FAT   89 CALORIES PER SERVING

> 24 small okra (about 1¼ pounds)
> 2 tablespoons plus 1 teaspoon red wine vinegar
> 1 teaspoon paprika
> 1 teaspoon Dijon mustard
> ½ teaspoon salt
> ⅛ teaspoon freshly ground pepper
> 2 tablespoons canola or olive oil
> 2 tablespoons reduced-sodium chicken broth
> 6 Boston or romaine lettuce leaves

1. Retain the point of the okra and trim the stem end to slightly resemble a pencil point. Place in a medium saucepan and add enough cold water to cover. Add 1 teaspoon of the vinegar and the paprika. Bring to a boil over high heat and cook until the okra are tender, 7 to 10 minutes. Drain into a colander, rinse under cold running water and transfer to paper towels to drain well.

2. In a small bowl, combine the mustard, salt and pepper. Whisk in the remaining 2 tablespoons vinegar. Slowly whisk in the oil and chicken broth and beat until well blended.

3. Place the okra in a medium bowl. Add the dressing and toss until well coated. Serve each guest 6 okra nestled on a lettuce leaf.

Pear Salad with Blue Cheese and Bitter Greens

In the South, greens are popular raw as well as cooked. Of course, the more tender varieties are used for salad, but we still like them with a bit of a bite. Chicory or watercress would be good choices here, though you could get fancy and try radicchio or frisée from the gourmet market. Pears and blue cheese are a classic combination, and low-calorie cream cheese makes this salad possible. Serve as a first course.

6 SERVINGS   49% CALORIES FROM FAT   167 CALORIES PER SERVING

> 1 teaspoon Dijon mustard
> 1/4 teaspoon salt
> 1/8 teaspoon freshly ground pepper
> 1 1/2 tablespoons red wine vinegar
> 2 tablespoons canola or safflower oil
> 1 1/2 ounces blue cheese, softened
> 2 ounces light cream cheese, softened
> 4 medium pears (about 1 1/2 pounds)
> 1 tablespoon lemon juice
> 2 cups bitter salad greens (see headnote)

1. In a small bowl, whisk together the mustard, salt, pepper and vinegar. Gradually whisk in the oil and beat until the dressing is well blended.

2. In another small bowl, combine the blue cheese and cream cheese. Mix and mash with a fork until smooth and creamy.

3. Peel and halve the pears. Use a small spoon to cut out the cores. Cut the pear halves into 3 wedges each. Brush the pear wedges with the lemon juice to prevent discoloration.

4. To serve, divide the greens among 6 salad plates. Arrange 4 pear wedges on each plate and top each with about 1 tablespoon of the cheese mixture. Drizzle about 2 teaspoons of the dressing over each salad and serve at once.

Down-Home Potato Salad

6 Servings   27% Calories from fat   136 Calories per serving

4 medium all-purpose potatoes (about 2 pounds)
¼ cup reduced-calorie mayonnaise
¼ cup reduced-calorie sour cream
½ teaspoon salt
¼ teaspoon freshly ground pepper
1 celery rib, thinly sliced
1 scallion, thinly sliced
1 tablespoon chopped parsley

1. Place the potatoes in a large pot of salted water and bring to a boil. Reduce the heat to medium and cook until tender, about 45 minutes. Set aside until cool enough to handle. Peel the potatoes and cut them into ½-inch cubes.

2. In a large bowl, combine the mayonnaise, sour cream, salt and pepper. Stir until well blended. Add the potatoes, celery, scallion and parsley. Stir gently to combine. Cover and refrigerate for at least 2 hours, or overnight, until chilled.

Low Country Rice Salad

As the rice salad chills with the mayonnaise, it will congeal enough to stay solid when inverted onto a platter for serving. Surround with quartered tomatoes or lots of green, leafy lettuce.

6 SERVINGS   17% CALORIES FROM FAT   165 CALORIES PER SERVING

> *1 cup long-grain white rice*
> *½ teaspoon salt*
> *½ medium green bell pepper, finely diced*
> *½ medium red or yellow bell pepper, finely diced*
> *1 small Vidalia onion, finely chopped*
> *1 medium tomato, peeled, seeded and chopped*
> *¼ cup reduced-calorie mayonnaise*
> *¼ cup low-fat plain yogurt*
> *2 teaspoons fresh lemon juice*
> *¼ teaspoon freshly ground pepper*

1. Bring 2 cups water to a boil in a medium saucepan. Add the rice and ¼ teaspoon salt. Reduce the heat to medium-low, cover and cook about 20 minutes. Remove from the heat, transfer to a bowl and let cool to room temperature.

2. In a large bowl, combine the green bell pepper, red bell pepper, onion, tomato, mayonnaise, yogurt and lemon juice. Stir in the rice and season with the pepper and the remaining ¼ teaspoon salt. Transfer the rice salad to a 1-quart mixing bowl or soufflé dish. Pack tightly with the back of a spoon or with a rubber spatula to compress. Cover and refrigerate for at least 2 hours or overnight, to chill and set.

3. Just before serving, invert the bowl onto a round platter to unmold. Smooth out any rough spots with a knife or rubber spatula, garnish as desired and serve.

Summer Stuffed Tomato Salad

Tomatoes are plentiful long into the fall months in the South. Cool and soothing, this salad makes a great first course or light lunch.

4 SERVINGS   24% CALORIES FROM FAT   135 CALORIES PER SERVING

> *4 medium tomatoes*
> *Salt and freshly ground pepper*
> *2 cups low-fat cottage cheese*
> *2 tablespoons reduced-calorie mayonnaise*
> *2 scallions, thinly sliced*
> *½ medium green bell pepper, finely chopped*
> *1 celery rib, thinly sliced*
> *1 tablespoon chopped parsley*

1. Core the tomatoes and cut them partially into quarters, stopping about ¼ inch from the bottom. Gently pull apart the sections to open up the center while leaving the tomato intact. Season with salt and pepper to taste.

2. In a medium bowl, combine the cottage cheese, mayonnaise, scallions, bell pepper and celery. Mix well. Season with salt and pepper to taste.

3. Mound the cottage cheese salad into the tomatoes, dividing evenly. Sprinkle the parsley over the top.

Chapter Three

CHICKEN, TURKEY, CORNISH HENS AND QUAIL

One of my favorite memories is standing knee-high to a big swaying skirt in the kitchen of my youth watching chicken being fried. I remember huge hands pulling flour-coated pieces of chicken from a plain brown paper bag and gently lowering them into giant iron skillets, the room filling with the most wonderful smells. The activity of setting the table and preparing the noonday meal evoked a sense that everything was right in the world.

Most of the chickens we consume these days come from somewhere in the South. The chicken-processing business is a thriving industry, providing lots of fresh, young broilers for everyone. As in the rest of the nation, Southern consumption of chicken has increased manyfold recently as the amount of red meat we eat declines. It isn't difficult to understand why. Chicken is a good source of protein, full of flavor and quite lean—if you remove the skin. For those of us who are interested in reducing the amount of fat in our diet and shaving off a few calories, chicken is an excellent choice.

Many of the recipes in this chapter call for skinless, boneless chicken breasts complemented by a wide variety of traditional Southern ingredients, such as squash, sweet potatoes, peppers, mushrooms, bourbon, pecans and greens. These down-home favorites are used to provide flavor and a contrast of textures and to add extra substance to the lean, white chicken.

I have also provided two "fried" chicken recipes. By removing the skin, coating the chicken pieces in bread crumbs and baking them in a hot oven, I've cut down on fat and retained the old-time flavor with less than half the calories. Egg whites and dry bread crumbs are used in one recipe, while buttermilk is used in the other. Results in both cases are excellent: crunchy on the outside and tender on the inside. Little seems to be lost in the translation to light.

It used to be that turkey was served only at Thanksgiving. Today, fresh turkey and turkey parts are found in supermarkets throughout the country all year round. Like chicken, it is an excellent lean, lower-cholesterol alternative to red meat. Virginia Braised Turkey Legs and Honey Mustard and Bourbon Glazed Turkey Breast make use of some fine Southern ingredients to create dishes that are authentic in flavor and light at the same time.

For festive dishes, Cornish Hens with Whiskey Glaze and Cornbread Stuffed Cornish Game Hens hearken back to the old South and make good use of familiar country ingredients. Wild-game hunting is still a popular sport in the South. Quail, dove and wild turkey are delicacies. Quail is the easiest to find in today's marketplace. Both Baked Quail Marinated in Buttermilk and Rosemary and Sherry Glazed Quail show how easy these small lean birds are to prepare and how delicious they are to eat.

New Orleans Chicken with Garlic

The amount of garlic in this recipe sounds like it might make a dinner companion turn his or her head if conversation takes place too soon after eating. Don't fret! Garlic becomes quite mild after it cooks. Folks in New Orleans swear that garlic is good for blood circulation, too. Once the garlic is passed through the sieve, the pulp helps to thicken the sauce as well as give it a unique, rich flavor. Serve with rice and stewed or fried okra.

4 SERVINGS   30% CALORIES FROM FAT   198 CALORIES PER SERVING

> *4 skinless, boneless chicken breast halves, 4 to 6 ounces each*
> *½ teaspoon salt*
> *¼ teaspoon freshly ground pepper*
> *1 tablespoon butter*
> *1½ teaspoons vegetable oil*
> *10 unpeeled garlic cloves*
> *1 cup reduced-sodium canned chicken broth*

1. Season the chicken with the salt and pepper. In a large nonstick skillet, melt the butter in the oil over medium-high heat. Add the chicken and cook, turning once, until lightly browned, about 5 minutes. Remove the chicken to a plate and set aside. Pour off any fat from the skillet; wipe out with paper towels.

2. With the back of a large knife, slightly crush the unpeeled garlic cloves. Put the crushed garlic in the skillet, add the broth and bring to a simmer. Reduce the heat to medium, return the chicken to the skillet, partially cover and cook until the chicken is slightly firm to the touch, about 10 minutes. With tongs, remove the chicken to a plate and cover with foil to keep warm.

3. Pour the contents of the skillet into a sieve over a medium bowl. With the back of a spoon, press the garlic through the sieve. Return the garlic sauce and chicken to the skillet and reheat gently over low heat. Serve on individual plates with the sauce spooned over the chicken.

Oven-Fried Chicken

In this lightened version of the old-fashioned Southern favorite, egg whites and dry bread crumbs take the place of oil in producing a crisp crust. Salt and pepper are the only seasonings for purists like me. If you prefer a more highly spiced recipe, take a look at Buttermilk "Fried" Chicken with Herbs, which follows.

4 SERVINGS   29% CALORIES FROM FAT   379 CALORIES PER SERVING

> *Vegetable cooking spray*
> *2 egg whites*
> *1 cup dry bread crumbs*
> *½ teaspoon salt*
> *½ teaspoon freshly ground pepper*
> *1 chicken, 3½ pounds, cut into 8 pieces, skin removed*

1. Preheat the oven to 350° F. Coat a nonstick baking sheet with vegetable cooking spray. In a shallow bowl or baking dish, combine the egg whites with 2 teaspoons water and beat with a fork to blend. In a separate bowl or dish, season the bread crumbs with the salt and pepper.

2. Rinse the chicken pieces and pat dry with paper towels. Dip each piece in the egg whites, letting the excess drip back into the bowl. Dredge in the bread crumbs, turning to coat all over.

3. Place the chicken on the prepared baking sheet and bake 45 minutes, or until golden brown and crispy.

Buttermilk "Fried" Chicken with Herbs

Buttermilk gives chicken a delightfully cheesy taste without a lot of fat. Rosemary, oregano or marjoram can be used in place of the thyme called for here.

4 SERVINGS   11% CALORIES FROM FAT   263 CALORIES PER SERVING

4 skinless, boneless chicken breast halves, 4 to 6 ounces each
1 cup buttermilk
1 cup dry bread crumbs
½ teaspoon dried thyme leaves
½ teaspoon salt
¼ teaspoon freshly ground black pepper
¼ teaspoon cayenne pepper

1. Place the chicken breasts in a nonreactive baking dish and pour the buttermilk over them. Cover and refrigerate at least 2 hours or overnight, turning occasionally.

2. Preheat the oven to 350° F. Place the bread crumbs in a shallow bowl. Add the thyme, salt, black pepper and cayenne and toss to mix. Remove the chicken from the buttermilk, drain slightly and roll in the seasoned bread crumbs to coat. Transfer to a nonstick baking sheet.

3. Bake the chicken 35 to 40 minutes, or until lightly browned. Serve at once.

—— *Chicken Breasts with Bourbon and Pecans* ——

Bourbon gives a fine flavor to this simple chicken dish. Be careful when adding bourbon to a hot skillet: it can go up in flames if not poured in off the heat. Serve with baked acorn squash or pureed sweet potatoes.

4 Servings   32% Calories from fat   186 Calories per serving

> *4 skinless, boneless chicken breast halves, 4 to 6 ounces each*
> *½ teaspoon salt*
> *¼ teaspoon freshly ground pepper*
> *1½ teaspoons butter*
> *1½ teaspoons vegetable oil*
> *¼ cup bourbon*
> *½ cup reduced-sodium canned chicken broth*
> *1½ tablespoons chopped pecans*

1. Season the chicken with the salt and pepper. In a large nonstick skillet, melt the butter in the oil over medium-high heat. Add the chicken and cook, turning once, until lightly browned, about 5 minutes. Transfer to a plate and cover with foil to keep warm.

2. Pour off any fat left in the skillet. Off heat, pour in the bourbon. Return the skillet to high heat and bring to a boil. Pour in the broth, return to a boil and add the chicken. Reduce the heat to low, partially cover and cook, turning occasionally, 3 minutes longer. Serve hot, spooning the pan juices over the chicken. Garnish with the chopped pecans.

Charleston Chicken Creole

4 SERVINGS   25% CALORIES FROM FAT   196 CALORIES PER SERVING

> 1 tablespoon olive oil
> 1 garlic clove, minced
> 1 small onion, thinly sliced
> 1 celery rib, thinly sliced
> 1 medium green bell pepper, finely diced
> 2 medium tomatoes, chopped, or 1 can (16 ounces) whole peeled
>   tomatoes, drained and chopped
> 1 bay leaf
> ½ teaspoon salt
> ⅛ teaspoon cayenne pepper
> 4 skinless, boneless chicken breast halves, 4 to 6 ounces each

1. Preheat the oven to 350° F. In a large skillet, heat the oil over medium heat. Add the garlic, onion, celery and bell pepper. Cook, stirring occasionally, until tender, about 4 minutes. Add the tomatoes, bay leaf, salt and cayenne. Cook the Creole sauce 3 minutes longer, stirring often.

2. Arrange the chicken breasts in an 8 × 11-inch baking dish. Pour the Creole sauce over the chicken.

3. Bake 15 to 20 minutes, until the chicken is tender and white throughout.

South Carolina Chicken and Rice with Saffron

Saffron adds a subtle flavor and gives a beautiful color to this Low Country dish. Serve with steamed broccoli and broiled tomatoes.

4 SERVINGS   14% CALORIES FROM FAT   357 CALORIES PER SERVING

1 tablespoon butter
1 medium onion, chopped
1/2 medium red bell pepper, chopped
1 garlic clove, minced
2 cups reduced-sodium canned chicken broth
1 small pinch of saffron threads (about 1/4 teaspoon)
1 cup long-grain white rice
1/2 teaspoon salt
1/4 teaspoon freshly ground pepper
1 1/4 pounds skinless, boneless chicken breasts, cut into 1/2-inch chunks

1. In a large saucepan, melt the butter over medium-high heat. Add the onion, red pepper and garlic. Cook, stirring frequently, until the onion is softened and translucent, about 3 minutes.

2. Pour in the chicken broth and saffron. Raise the heat to high and bring to a boil. Stir in the rice and season with the salt and pepper. Reduce the heat to low, cover and cook 10 minutes.

3. Add the chicken to the pan and continue to cook, covered, until the rice and chicken are tender, 8 to 10 minutes longer.

Chicken and Summer Squash

4 Servings   32% Calories from fat   231 Calories per serving

4 skinless, boneless chicken breast halves, 4 to 6 ounces each
½ teaspoon salt
¼ teaspoon freshly ground pepper
1 tablespoon butter
1 tablespoon vegetable oil
¾ pound yellow (summer) squash, sliced
¾ pound zucchini, sliced
1 medium tomato, peeled, seeded and chopped

1. Season the chicken with half the salt and half the pepper. In a large non-stick skillet, melt the butter in the oil over medium-high heat. Add the chicken and cook, turning, until lightly browned, about 2 minutes per side. Transfer to a large plate or platter and cover to keep warm.

2. Pour off the fat from the skillet. Add the squash, zucchini and tomato and season with the remaining salt and pepper. Cook over medium-high heat, stirring often, until the squash is slightly softened, about 3 minutes. Return the chicken to the skillet. Reduce the heat to medium and cook, partially covered, until the squash is soft and the chicken is white throughout but still juicy, about 5 minutes longer.

3. Transfer the chicken to a platter and cover with foil to keep warm. Raise the heat to high and cook the vegetable mixture, stirring often, until almost all the liquid has evaporated, about 2 minutes. Spoon the vegetables around the chicken and serve at once.

Shady Tree Lemon Chicken

4 Servings   23% Calories from fat   183 Calories per serving

1 tablespoon butter
4 skinless, boneless chicken breast halves, 4 to 6 ounces each
1 small onion, thinly sliced
1 teaspoon grated lemon zest
2 teaspoons honey
2 tablespoons fresh lemon juice
½ teaspoon salt
¼ teaspoon freshly ground pepper

1. Preheat the oven to 350° F. Spread the butter over the bottom of an 8 × 11-inch baking dish. Arrange the chicken in the dish and scatter the onion on top. Sprinkle on the lemon zest and drizzle the honey and lemon juice over the chicken. Season with the salt and pepper.

2. Bake 15 to 17 minutes, until the chicken is lightly browned and white throughout. Transfer to individual plates and spoon the pan juices over the chicken.

Chicken and Sweet Potato Hash

4 Servings   24% Calories from fat   294 Calories per serving

2 medium sweet potatoes, about 1¼ pounds
1 pound skinless, boneless chicken breasts
2 tablespoons butter
1 medium onion, finely chopped
½ cup reduced-sodium canned chicken broth
¼ teaspoon salt
¼ teaspoon freshly ground pepper

1. Peel the sweet potatoes and cut them into ½-inch cubes. Cut the chicken into ½-inch chunks.

2. In a large nonstick skillet, melt the butter over medium-high heat. Add the onion and cook, stirring frequently, until translucent, about 2 minutes. Stir in the sweet potatoes. Reduce the heat to medium-low, partially cover and cook, stirring often, until slightly softened, about 10 minutes.

3. Add the chicken, broth, salt and pepper. Bring to a boil over high heat. Cook, stirring constantly, until almost all the liquid has evaporated, the sweet potatoes are tender and the chicken is firm, 3 to 5 minutes longer.

Glazed Chicken with White Turnips

4 SERVINGS   21% CALORIES FROM FAT   199 CALORIES PER SERVING

1 pound turnips, peeled and quartered
2 teaspoons sugar
1 tablespoon butter
¼ teaspoon salt
¼ teaspoon freshly ground pepper
1¼ pounds skinless, boneless chicken breasts, cut into 1-inch pieces
1 tablespoon chopped parsley

1. In a large nonstick skillet, combine the turnips, sugar, butter, salt, pepper and ¾ cup water. Cook over medium heat, stirring and tossing frequently, until the water is evaporated and the turnips are almost tender, 8 to 10 minutes. (Sugar burns easily, so watch carefully and lower the heat if necessary. Scrape from the bottom of the skillet to produce an even browning and prevent scorching.)

2. Add the chicken pieces, reduce the heat to medium and cook, stirring constantly, until the chicken is firm, white throughout and lightly glazed and the turnips are tender and browned, about 5 minutes. Garnish with the parsley and serve at once.

Chicken Roulades with Mustard Greens

4 SERVINGS   22% CALORIES FROM FAT   217 CALORIES PER SERVING

½ pound mustard greens, tough stems removed
2 tablespoons grated onion
2 tablespoons low-fat cottage cheese
¼ cup fat-free cracker crumbs
½ teaspoon salt
¼ teaspoon freshly ground pepper
4 skinless, boneless chicken breast halves, 4 to 6 ounces each
1 tablespoon vegetable oil
Paprika

1. Bring a large pot of salted water to a boil. Add the mustard greens and cook over high heat until slightly tender, about 3 minutes. Drain well.

2. In a food processor, puree the greens until finely chopped. Add the onion, cottage cheese, cracker crumbs, salt and pepper and pulse until smooth.

3. Preheat the oven to 350° F. With the back of a large knife or a rolling pin, pound the chicken breasts between 2 pieces of wax paper until ¼ inch thick. Spread 2 heaping tablespoons of the mustard green mixture in the center of each chicken breast. Bring the opposite ends of the chicken to the center, overlapping slightly to enclose the filling.

4. Arrange the roulades, seam side-down, in a nonstick 8- or 9-inch square baking dish. Brush the roulades lightly with oil, dust with paprika and bake 15 minutes, or until lightly browned and slightly firm to the touch. Cut into ½-inch-thick slices and arrange attractively on individual serving plates.

Chicken with Tomatoes, Peppers and Fresh Basil

4 SERVINGS   25% CALORIES FROM FAT   189 CALORIES PER SERVING

1 tablespoon vegetable oil
1 small onion, thinly sliced
1 medium red bell pepper, thinly sliced
1 large tomato, finely chopped
½ cup shredded fresh basil or 2 tablespoons chopped parsley mixed with
   1 teaspoon dried basil
4 skinless, boneless chicken breast halves, 4 to 6 ounces each
½ teaspoon salt
¼ teaspoon freshly ground pepper

1. Preheat the oven to 350° F. In a large nonstick skillet, heat the oil over medium heat. Add the onion and bell pepper and cook, stirring occasionally, until tender, 3 to 4 minutes. Add the tomato and basil and cook the sauce 2 minutes longer.

2. Season the chicken with the salt and pepper and place in an 8 × 11-baking dish. Pour the sauce over the chicken and bake 15 to 20 minutes, until the chicken is white throughout but still juicy.

Georgia Chicken Salad with Mint and Toasted Pecans

Cool, main-course salads are a popular item in the steamy South, whether for luncheon, a light supper or as part of a buffet. Here mint and toasted pecans add inimitable regional flavor to a dish that's popular everywhere.

6 SERVINGS   34% CALORIES FROM FAT   230 CALORIES PER SERVING

1 whole chicken, 3½ pounds
1 medium onion, quartered
1 medium carrot, coarsely chopped
1 whole celery rib, quartered, plus 2 tablespoons chopped celery
¼ cup pecans
2 tablespoons chopped scallions
1 tablespoon chopped fresh mint or ½ teaspoon dried
¼ cup reduced-calorie mayonnaise
¼ cup nonfat plain yogurt
¼ teaspoon salt
¼ teaspoon freshly ground pepper

1. Rinse the chicken well inside and out under cold running water and place in a soup kettle. Add the onion, carrot and celery rib. Pour in enough cold water to cover. Bring to a boil over high heat, skimming occasionally. Reduce the heat to medium and cook until the chicken is very tender, about 45 minutes. Remove the chicken to a plate and set aside to cool. (Strain the stock and save for another use. It can be substituted for canned chicken broth in any recipe in the soup chapter.)

2. Meanwhile, preheat the oven to 350° F. Spread out the pecans in a small baking dish and toast in the oven until fragrant and lightly browned, about 5 minutes. Immediately transfer to a small plate and let cool. Chop the pecans.

3. When the chicken is cool enough to handle, remove the meat from the bones, discarding all the skin and fat. Cut the meat into 1-inch chunks.

4. In a medium bowl, combine the chopped celery, scallions, mint, mayonnaise, yogurt, salt and pepper. Stir until well blended. Add the chicken chunks and chopped toasted pecans. Toss until mixed evenly. Cover and refrigerate at least 2 hours, or overnight, until chilled before serving.

Honey Mustard and Bourbon Glazed Turkey Breast

Whole turkey breasts are an economical and healthy choice for the home cook. There is little waste, the tender white meat is light in fat and calories and it is wonderful for sandwiches if any is left over.

Honey mustard, which is available in many supermarkets and in specialty food shops, is a relatively new product that combines two familiar Southern flavors. The bourbon helps thin out the mustard for brushing, and it adds a little kick to the dish that folks below the Mason-Dixon line tend to appreciate. Serve the breast sliced thin, with sweet potatoes and green beans.

8 TO 10 SERVINGS   17% CALORIES FROM FAT   257 CALORIES PER SERVING

> *1 fresh turkey breast, bone in, about 5½ pounds*
> *Vegetable cooking spray*
> *½ cup honey mustard*
> *¼ cup bourbon*
> *½ cup reduced-sodium canned chicken broth or water*

1. Preheat the oven to 350° F. Remove the skin from the turkey breast. Coat the bottom of a large roasting pan with vegetable cooking spray. Set the turkey breast, bone side-down, in the pan.

2. In a small mixing bowl, stir together the mustard and bourbon until smooth. Brush half of this mixture evenly over the turkey. Pour the broth into the pan around it. Tent the turkey breast with foil.

3. Roast in the oven, basting occasionally with the remaining bourbon-mustard mixture and with the accumulated pan juices, about 1½ hours, or until golden brown. Remove the foil during the last 20 minutes of cooking for darker browning. Check frequently during cooking to ensure that there is enough liquid in the bottom of the roasting pan to prevent scorching. Add additional broth or water as needed to keep a constant film of liquid in the pan. Let the turkey rest for 5 to 10 minutes before slicing to allow the meat to firm up and the juices to be absorbed.

Jambalaya

Jambalaya is a spicy dish served in the Mississippi Delta, where good eating and festive living are a way of life. This recipe uses less rice than some versions for a lighter dish. Sausage made from turkey has a wonderful flavor and is much lower in fat and cholesterol than the pork-based variety. Serve with a green salad and fresh tomatoes.

6 SERVINGS   29% CALORIES FROM FAT   287 CALORIES PER SERVING

> 2 tablespoons canola or safflower oil
> 1 medium onion, finely chopped
> 1 green bell pepper, finely chopped
> 1 celery rib, thinly sliced
> 1 garlic clove, minced
> 2 medium tomatoes, peeled, seeded and chopped
> 1 cup long-grain white rice
> 1½ cups reduced-sodium canned chicken broth
> Several drops of hot pepper sauce or to taste
> 1 teaspoon fresh thyme leaves or ½ teaspoon dried
> 1 bay leaf
> ½ teaspoon salt
> ¼ teaspoon freshly ground black pepper
> ¼ teaspoon cayenne pepper
> ½ pound turkey spicy Italian or Polish kielbasa-type sausage, cut into
>   ¼-inch-thick slices
> ¼ pound skinless, boneless chicken breast, cut into 1-inch pieces
> Vegetable cooking spray
> ½ pound medium shrimp, shelled, deveined and cut into 1-inch pieces
> 1 tablespoon chopped parsley

1. In a large nonstick saucepan or flameproof casserole, heat the oil over medium heat. Add the onion, pepper, celery and garlic. Cover and cook 2 minutes, stirring often. Uncover and continue to cook, until softened, about 3 minutes longer. Stir in the tomatoes, rice and chicken broth. Add the hot sauce, thyme, bay leaf, salt, black pepper and cayenne. Reduce the heat to medium-low, cover and cook for 20 minutes.

2. Meanwhile, place the sausage and chicken in a medium nonstick skillet coated with vegetable cooking spray. Cook over medium heat, turning, until lightly browned and firm to the touch, about 5 minutes.

3. Gently stir the rice to fluff. Add the chicken, kielbasa and shrimp to the saucepan. Return to medium heat and cook for 5 minutes. Stir gently, cover and cook 5 minutes longer. Transfer to a large serving bowl and serve at once, sprinkled with the parsley.

—— *Lemon-Rosemary Roasted Turkey Breast* ——

Lemon and rosemary are sophisticated Southern flavors that blend well with turkey. We've removed the skin from the breast to reduce fat. The spicy coating helps to protect the meat as it cooks. For extra flavor, coat the breast with the paste and refrigerate for 2 to 3 hours before roasting. Carve into thin slices and serve with cornbread stuffing on page 74.

8 to 10 Servings   23% Calories from fat   245 Calories per serving

> 1 fresh turkey breast, bone in, about 5½ pounds
> Vegetable cooking spray
> 2 pieces of lemon zest, 2 inches long
> 1 teaspoon black peppercorns
> ½ teaspoon coarse salt
> ½ teaspoon sugar
> 2 teaspoons chopped fresh rosemary or 1 teaspoon dried
> 1 garlic clove, halved
> 1 tablespoon canola or safflower oil

1. Preheat the oven to 350° F. Remove the skin from the turkey breast and pat dry with paper towels. Coat a medium roasting pan with vegetable cooking spray.

2. In an electric spice grinder or mortar and pestle, combine the lemon zest, peppercorns, salt, sugar, rosemary and garlic. Grind into a fine powder and empty into a small bowl. Stir in the oil to form a paste. Rub the turkey all over with the paste and set, bone side-down, in the prepared roasting pan.

3. Roast 1½ hours, or until there are no traces of pink and the breast is well browned. Let stand for 20 minutes before carving.

Dirty Rice

The name for this popular Louisiana dish has nothing to do with cleanliness. It comes from the muddy color of the rice, which is darkened by the addition of ground meats and traditionally with liver and giblets. For a leaner version, I've used ground turkey in place of beef or pork. Serve with a leafy green salad and seasonal vegetables.

4 SERVINGS   30% CALORIES FROM FAT   352 CALORIES PER SERVING

> 1 cup long-grain white rice
> 2 cups reduced-sodium canned chicken broth
> 2 teaspoons butter
> 2 teaspoons canola or safflower oil
> 1 onion, finely chopped
> 1 garlic clove, minced
> 1 celery rib, thinly sliced
> ½ medium green bell pepper, finely chopped
> ¾ pound ground turkey
> 1 teaspoon fresh thyme leaves or ½ teaspoon dried
> ¼ teaspoon salt
> ¼ teaspoon freshly ground pepper
> ⅛ teaspoon cayenne pepper
> 1 tablespoon chopped parsley

1. In a medium saucepan, combine the rice and chicken broth. Bring to a boil over high heat. Reduce the heat to medium-low, cover and cook 20 minutes, until the rice is tender and all the liquid has been absorbed.

2. Meanwhile, melt the butter in the oil in a large nonstick skillet over medium-high heat. Add the onion, garlic, celery and green pepper. Cook, stirring often, until softened, about 5 minutes. Add the turkey, season with the thyme, salt, pepper and cayenne. Cook, stirring often to break up any lumps of meat, until the turkey is tender and has lost all traces of pink, 5 to 7 minutes.

3. Add the rice to the turkey mixture and stir to blend. Cook over low heat, stirring, until the rice is hot and the flavors are blended, 2 to 3 minutes. Season with additional salt and pepper to taste. Transfer to a serving bowl, garnish with the parsley and serve at once.

Turkey Croquettes

Use leftover turkey to make crispy croquettes. Egg whites and just a dab of reduced-calorie mayonnaise keep these light. Serve with tomato sauce and a green salad for a light lunch.

4 Servings   31% Calories from fat   242 Calories per serving

> 2 cups cooked white turkey meat
> 2 egg whites
> ²/₃ cup plain dry bread crumbs
> 1 tablespoon reduced-calorie mayonnaise
> 1 tablespoon Dijon mustard
> 1 medium celery rib, finely chopped
> 1 medium onion, finely chopped
> 1 tablespoon chopped fresh sage or 1 teaspoon dried
> ½ teaspoon salt
> ¼ teaspoon freshly ground pepper
> 1 tablespoon canola or safflower oil

1. In a food processor, pulse the turkey until coarsely ground. In a large bowl, combine the turkey with the egg whites, bread crumbs, mayonnaise, mustard, celery, onion, sage, salt and pepper. Stir to blend well. Use your hands to shape the mixture into 4 round patties and set aside.

2. In a large nonstick skillet, heat the oil over medium heat. Add the turkey patties and cook, turning once, until golden brown outside and cooked through with no trace of pink in the center, about 3 minutes on each side. Serve hot.

Virginia Braised Turkey Legs

Turkey has long been popular in the South. Most folks prefer the white meat and overlook the rich flavor of the legs and thighs. This recipe treats the legs as Europeans do lamb shanks. Long, slow cooking breaks down the tough fibers and leaves a meltingly good piece of lean meat. Serve with rice, noodles or mashed potatoes and a green vegetable.

4 SERVINGS   30% CALORIES FROM FAT   164 CALORIES PER SERVING

> *4 turkey legs, about ½ pound each*
> *Vegetable cooking spray*
> *½ teaspoon salt*
> *¼ teaspoon freshly ground pepper*
> *2 carrots, finely chopped*
> *1 celery rib, thinly sliced*
> *1 medium onion, finely chopped*
> *1 large tomato, coarsely chopped*
> *1 cup reduced-sodium canned chicken broth or water*
> *1 tablespoon chopped fresh marjoram or 1 teaspoon dried*

1. Preheat the oven to 325° F. Pull the skin off the turkey legs. Trim off any fat you see. Spray the bottom of a large flameproof casserole with vegetable cooking spray. Season the turkey legs with the salt and pepper. Cook the legs over medium heat, turning frequently, until lightly browned, about 2 minutes. Remove and set aside.

2. Add the carrots, celery and onion to the casserole. Cook, stirring, until the onion is softened, 2 to 3 minutes. Add the tomato, broth and marjoram and bring to a simmer. Return the turkey legs to the casserole, cover and cook in the oven about 1½ hours, or until the turkey is very tender. Add additional liquid if needed to prevent scorching. Remove the legs to a platter to cool.

3. Set a sieve over a medium saucepan and pour in the vegetables and cooking liquid from the casserole. Press down on the vegetables to extract as much liquid as possible. There should be 1 cup. If not, add enough chicken broth or water to measure this amount. Skim all the fat off the broth.

4. When the legs are cool enough to handle, pull the meat away from the bones, discarding all skin, fat, tendons and gristle. Cut the meat into large chunks. Add the turkey to the saucepan with the strained cooking liquid and gently reheat over low heat.

Cornish Hens with Whiskey Glaze

Ask your butcher to split the hens for broiling, removing the backbones. Serve with greens and baked sweet potatoes.

4 SERVINGS   49% CALORIES FROM FAT   356 CALORIES PER SERVING

> 2 small Cornish game hens, 1¼ to 1½ pounds each, halved
> ½ teaspoon salt
> ¼ teaspoon freshly ground pepper
> ½ cup whiskey
> 2 tablespoons dark brown sugar
> 1 teaspoon Dijon mustard

1. Preheat the oven to 375° F. Season the hens with the salt and pepper. Place skin side-up in a large baking dish.

2. In a small bowl, whisk together the whiskey, brown sugar and mustard. Pour over the hens.

3. Place in the upper third of the oven and roast, basting frequently with the pan juices, about 30 minutes, until the hens are browned outside and the juices run clear when the thigh is pierced with the tip of a small knife.

Cornbread Stuffed Cornish Game Hens

4 Servings 53% Calories from fat 378 Calories per serving

1 tablespoon butter
1 medium celery rib, thinly sliced
1 small onion, finely chopped
1 cup finely crumbled day-old cornbread or fresh bread crumbs
1½ tablespoons chopped pecans
½ cup reduced-sodium canned chicken broth or water
½ teaspoon salt
¼ teaspoon freshly ground pepper
2 small Cornish game hens, 1¼ pounds each

1. Preheat the oven to 425° F. In a large nonstick skillet, melt the butter over medium-high heat. Add the celery and onion and cook, stirring often, until softened, 2 to 3 minutes. Remove from the heat. Stir in the cornbread and pecans and pour in ¼ cup of the chicken broth. Season with the salt and pepper.

2. Place half of the stuffing into the main cavity of each hen and set the birds breast side-up in a large baking dish. Pour the remaining ¼ cup broth over the hens; cover loosely with foil.

3. Roast the hens, basting frequently with the pan juices, 10 minutes. Remove the foil and continue roasting and basting, until the birds are well browned and their juices run clear when a thigh is pierced with the tip of a small knife, 30 to 35 minutes longer.

Tupelo Honey Cornish Hens

Tupelo honey comes from the flower of the tupelo tree, known in some parts of the South as the sour gum tree. This is a popular Southern honey with a distinctive but subtle floral flavor, reminiscent of cloves or lavender. Clove, wildflower or any other good honey can be substituted.

4 SERVINGS   54% CALORIES FROM FAT   382 CALORIES PER SERVING

> 2 small Cornish game hens, about 1¼ pounds each, halved
> ½ teaspoon salt
> ¼ teaspoon freshly ground pepper
> 2 tablespoons butter
> 2 tablespoons Tupelo honey

1. Preheat the oven to 375° F. Season the hens with the salt and pepper. Place skin side-up in a large baking dish.

2. In a small saucepan, melt the butter with the honey over low heat, stirring until smooth. Pour the honey butter over the game hens.

3. Bake, basting frequently with the pan juices, until the hens are browned and their juices run clear when a thigh is pierced with the tip of a small knife, about 30 minutes.

— *Baked Quail Marinated in Buttermilk and* — *Rosemary*

Serve with baked grits and a green salad for a Sunday brunch.

4 Servings   56% Calories from fat   331 Calories per serving

> 2 cups buttermilk
> 1 garlic clove, minced
> 2 tablespoons chopped fresh rosemary or 2 teaspoons dried
> ½ teaspoon salt
> ¼ teaspoon freshly ground pepper
> 12 partially boned quail (see headnote on page 77), thawed if frozen

1. In a large bowl, combine the buttermilk, garlic, rosemary, salt and pepper. Stir well to blend. Place the quail in a single layer in a large baking dish or shallow bowl. Pour the buttermilk over the birds, cover with plastic wrap and marinate in the refrigerator, turning often, 3 to 4 hours or overnight.

2. Preheat the oven to 450° F. Remove the quail from the marinade and place breast side-down on a baking sheet. Roast 20 to 25 minutes, or until lightly browned. Turn over and cook for 5 minutes on the other side. Serve at once.

Sherry Glazed Quail

Quail are elegant small birds and a treat for most people, but eating them can be difficult. To make life easier for guests and to facilitate the marinating, the following recipe calls for partially boned quail. Frozen quail are often sold already boned. If you're using fresh quail, ask your butcher to bone the birds for you. To do it yourself, simply cut away the backbone and remove the ribs, breastbone and wishbone. Cut each bird in half lengthwise, leaving the leg and thigh bone in. Cut off the wing tips at the elbow.

6 SERVINGS   54% CALORIES FROM FAT   345 CALORIES PER SERVING

> *12 partially boned quail (see headnote), thawed if frozen*
> *½ teaspoon salt*
> *¼ teaspoon freshly ground pepper*
> *1 cup dry sherry*
> *2 tablespoons dark brown sugar*
> *1 tablespoon canola or safflower oil*

1. Arrange the quail in a large, nonreactive baking dish and season with the salt and pepper. In a small bowl, combine the sherry with the brown sugar and oil. Stir until the sugar is dissolved. Pour the sherry mixture over the quail. Cover and marinate in the refrigerator at least 2 hours, turning often, or overnight.

2. Preheat the broiler or prepare a charcoal fire and let it burn down to a gray ash. Arrange the quail breast side-down in a single layer on a broiling pan (in 2 batches, if necessary) or breast side-up on the charcoal grill. Broil or grill 5 to 6 inches from the heat, basting often with the marinade, 12 to 15 minutes, until well browned, Turn over and broil or grill 5 minutes longer.

Chapter Four

BARBECUE
AND
OTHER
SOUTHERN
WAYS
WITH
MEAT

Barbecue is king in the American South. Every community boasts an establishment dedicated to the fine art of roasting and smoking meats to a lip-smacking, succulent tenderness. Big black pits burn hickory wood or light oak, which imparts a wonderful flavor as chunks of beef or pork cook slowly, swathed in a coat of spicy sauce. Served with Coleslaw (page 44) Brunswick Stew (page 26) and white bread, there is nothing that quite fits the appetites of hungry Southerners as does barbecue. Many of the recipes in this chapter can be done over a charcoal fire with only slight adaptations, an excellent way to cook with a minimum of added fat.

There are other ways to enjoy meat, too. Trimmed, lean cuts of beef can be nourishing, fortifying and nutritious when served in controlled portions. Rib steaks, tenderloin, sirloin, lean ground beef and flank steak are good choices for light fare. Broiling, grilling and sautéing are the cooking methods most used in this chapter. Quick cooking of tender cuts minimizes the use of added fat, seals in moisture and adds flavor. But I also had to include slow-cooking Louisiana Pot Roast with Okra and the old-time favorite from my part of Georgia—Southern Smothered Steak.

Frugal Southerners long ago developed an affinity for the pig. Easy to raise, economical to feed and capable of providing a family with many meals, pork has long been a part of the landscape below the Mason-Dixon line. Smoked, cured, salted and fresh pork are staples in this part of the world. Bacon, cracklins, pork rinds and country hams, all heavily cured and often smoked, remind us of a time before refrigeration when food was kept in smokehouses and dark cellars. The omnipresent pork fat was used to flavor everything from bread to vegetables.

Times have changed. Modern methods of raising pork have provided today's consumer with a product that is half as fatty as it was even 15 years ago. The other white meat, as it is called, has only about 200 calories and 9 grams of fat in a three-ounce serving. Most of the following recipes call for the tenderloin or the loin or center-cut loin chops. These are the least fatty and are by far the most tender of all the pork parts. These cuts have a tendency to dry out if overcooked, so pay close attention to cooking times.

It's important to remember that meat is only one part of the meal. Add vegetables, cornbread or biscuits, sweet potatoes, ice tea and cobbler and you have a typical Southern menu. For today's lifestyle, a greater variety of vegetable, bean and grain side dishes with less emphasis on meat is recommended. This is not meant to discourage the pleasure of eating meat, just to create a healthy diet with a balance of leaner, alternative sources of protein.

Southern Smothered Steak

Lean round steak takes to long, slow, moist cooking with aromatic seasonings. For added flavor and less sodium, the beef broth can be replaced with dry red wine or beer.

4 SERVINGS   29% CALORIES FROM FAT   245 CALORIES PER SERVING

1 pound well-trimmed, lean top round steak
¼ cup flour
1 tablespoon vegetable oil
2 onions, thinly sliced
1 cup beef broth
2 large ripe tomatoes, chopped, or 1 can (16 ounces) whole peeled
    tomatoes, drained and chopped
1 bay leaf
1 tablespoon chopped fresh parsley
1 tablespoon Worcestershire sauce
1 tablespoon lemon juice
¼ teaspoon Tabasco
½ teaspoon salt
¼ teaspoon freshly ground pepper

1. Dredge the steak in the flour and shake off any excess. In a large nonstick skillet, heat the oil over medium-high heat. Add the steak and cook, turning often, until browned, about 4 minutes. Remove to a platter and set aside.

2. Add the onions to the skillet and cook, stirring constantly to pick up any brown bits from the bottom of the pan, until slightly softened, about 2 minutes. Pour in the beef broth and add the tomatoes, bay leaf, parsley, Worcestershire sauce, lemon juice, Tabasco, salt and pepper. Return the steak to the skillet. Cover the pan, reduce the heat to medium-low and simmer 45 minutes to 1 hour, until the steak is tender and the sauce is thick.

3. To serve, cut the steak into thin slices. Remove the bay leaf from the skillet, tilt the pan and skim off all fat from the liquid. Spoon the pan juices and onions over the meat.

Spicy Minute Steaks

Because of its flavor and juiciness, chuck is the steak of choice in the South, but fillet steaks cut from the tenderloin provide a much lighter, leaner and more tender option. This recipe offers a simple but flavorful way to make this lean cut of meat a true Southern delight. Serve with collard greens or turnip greens and a slice of cornbread.

4 Servings   46% Calories from fat   189 Calories per serving

4 well-trimmed fillet steaks, cut ¾ inch thick, about 4 ounces each
4 teaspoons Dijon mustard
1 teaspoon fresh thyme leaves or ½ teaspoon dried
⅛ teaspoon cayenne pepper
¼ teaspoon salt
¼ teaspoon freshly ground pepper

1. Preheat the broiler. Arrange the steaks on a broiling pan. In a small bowl, combine the mustard, thyme, cayenne, salt and pepper. Stir to blend well. Spread the seasoned mustard evenly over the top of the steaks.

2. Broil about 4 inches from the heat without turning, 6 to 8 minutes, until the meat is browned outside and rare or medium-rare inside.

Peachtree Street Beef Kebabs

Serve kebabs with rice or corn on the cob and a green leafy salad. These are great done on the grill, too!

4 Servings   41% Calories from fat   247 Calories per serving

1¼ pounds well-trimmed flank steak, cut into 1½-inch cubes
2 tablespoons ketchup
1 tablespoon Worcestershire sauce
1 tablespoon Dijon mustard
2 teaspoons lemon juice
½ teaspoon salt

¼ teaspoon freshly ground pepper
1 medium red bell pepper, cut into 1-inch squares
1 medium yellow bell pepper, cut into 1-inch squares

1. Preheat the broiler. Place the beef in a medium bowl. In a small bowl, combine the ketchup, Worcestershire sauce, mustard, lemon juice, salt and pepper. Blend well and pour over the beef. Stir and toss until well coated.

2. On 4 long metal skewers, alternate the pieces of red and yellow pepper with the beef. Arrange on a broiling pan and broil 4 to 6 inches from the heat, turning often, 8 to 10 minutes, until the meat is browned and rare or medium-rare inside.

Barbecued Beef

Not all barbecue sauces are tomato based. This is a light, low-fat sauce that uses herbs and vinegar to pack that zesty punch Southerners like so much.

4 SERVINGS   40% CALORIES FROM FAT   184 CALORIES PER SERVING

½ cup white wine vinegar
1½ teaspoons canola or safflower oil
1 garlic clove, minced
½ teaspoon dried thyme leaves
⅛ teaspoon cayenne pepper
¼ teaspoon salt
⅛ teaspoon freshly ground black pepper
4 lean boneless top sirloin steaks, trimmed of all fat, cut ½ inch thick, about 4 ounces each

1. In a small bowl, combine the vinegar, oil, garlic, thyme, cayenne, salt and pepper. Mix well and pour into a nonreactive baking dish or shallow bowl. Place the steaks in the marinade and refrigerate, turning often, 2 hours or overnight.

2. Preheat the broiler. Remove the steaks from the marinade and arrange on a broiling pan. Broil about 4 inches from the heat, turning once, 6 to 8 minutes, or until cooked to desired degree of doneness. Alternatively, prepare a charcoal fire, let burn down to a gray ash and proceed as for broiling.

Smothered Beef with Herbed Onions and Mushrooms

Herbs lend an enhancing touch to this traditional recipe. Thyme and rosemary are just suggestions; use whatever is on hand, such as oregano, marjoram, chervil or parsley, particularly if it is fresh.

4 SERVINGS   36% CALORIES FROM FAT   259 CALORIES PER SERVING

4 boneless rib steaks, trimmed of all fat, cut about ½ inch thick, about 4 ounces each
½ teaspoon salt
¼ teaspoon freshly ground pepper
½ cup all-purpose flour
Vegetable cooking spray
4 medium mushrooms, thinly sliced
1 medium onion, thinly sliced
1 garlic clove, minced
1 teaspoon chopped fresh thyme or ½ teaspoon dried
1 teaspoon chopped fresh rosemary or ½ teaspoon dried
½ cup beef broth

1. Season the steaks with the salt and pepper. Dredge lightly in the flour to coat both sides; shake off the excess.

2. Coat the bottom of a large nonstick skillet with vegetable cooking spray and heat the skillet over medium-high heat. Add the steaks and cook, turning once, until browned, about 2 minutes per side. Remove to a plate and set aside.

3. Add the mushrooms, onion, garlic, thyme, rosemary and beef broth to the skillet and stir to mix. Cook, stirring often, until the onion is slightly softened, about 3 minutes. Return the steaks to the skillet, cover loosely with foil and cook over medium-high heat until tender, about 4 minutes.

4. Remove the steaks to a platter and cover with foil to keep warm. Raise the heat to high and boil the broth and the vegetables until the liquid is reduced by half, about 2 minutes. Spoon the sauce and vegetables over the beef and serve at once.

Galveston Grilled Flank Steak

When trimmed of any extra fat on the outside, flank steak is a relatively lean cut that should be cooked rare or it will be tough and tasteless. Slice thinly on the diagonal and serve with baked potatoes.

6 SERVINGS   44% CALORIES FROM FAT   186 CALORIES PER SERVING

1 flank steak, trimmed of all fat, about 1½ pounds
2 teaspoons mild chili powder, or more to taste
1 tablespoon ketchup
1 tablespoon Worcestershire sauce
1 garlic clove, minced

1. In a nonreactive baking dish large enough to hold the flank steak flat, mix together the chili powder with the ketchup, Worcestershire sauce, garlic and 2 tablespoons water to form a smooth paste. Brush both sides of the flank steak with this mixture and place in the dish. Cover and refrigerate for at least 2 hours or overnight.

2. Preheat the broiler. Transfer the steak to a broiling pan and broil 4 to 6 inches away from the heat, 4 to 5 minutes on each side, until rare or medium-rare. To serve, carve the steak crosswise on a diagonal into thin slices.

Louisiana Pot Roast with Okra

Red wine is often the cooking medium of choice in this French-inspired region of the country. Okra is the quintessential southern vegetable, but if the taste or texture is not to your liking, you can substitute sliced carrots or green beans or omit the vegetable entirely. Serve the roast with rice and a green salad. If you can afford the extra 100 calories for a slice, crusty bread is great for sopping up the sauce.

8 SERVINGS   29% CALORIES FROM FAT   292 CALORIES PER SERVING

3 pounds lean top round
1 medium onion, quartered
2 medium carrots, thickly sliced
1 celery rib, thickly sliced
Several sprigs of fresh thyme or 1 teaspoon dried thyme leaves
1 bay leaf
1 bottle (750 ml) hearty red wine, preferably Burgundy
½ teaspoon salt
¼ teaspoon freshly ground pepper
2 tablespoons vegetable oil
2 tablespoons flour
1 pound okra, cut into ¼-inch slices

1. Place the roast in a large bowl. Surround with the onion, carrots, celery, thyme and bay leaf. Pour on the wine. Cover and marinate in the refrigerator, at least 24 and up to 48 hours.

2. Preheat the oven to 350° F. Remove the roast from the marinade and pat dry with paper towels. Season with the salt and pepper. Strain the marinade; reserve the vegetables and liquid separately.

3. In a large flameproof casserole, heat the oil over medium-high heat. Add the roast and cook, turning often, until browned all over, 5 to 7 minutes. Transfer to a plate and set aside. Add the vegetables from the marinade to the casserole and sprinkle on the flour. Cook, stirring constantly, until lightly browned, about 2 minutes. Pour in the liquid from the marinade, raise the heat to high and bring to a boil, scraping up the brown bits from the bottom of the pan. Return the roast to the casserole and cover. Transfer to the oven and cook 2½ to 3 hours, or until the meat is very tender.

4. Bring a medium saucepan of salted water to a boil over high heat. Add the okra and cook until barely tender, 3 to 5 minutes. Drain and rinse under cold, running water. Drain well.

5. Remove the meat to a cutting board and cover loosely with foil. Strain the cooking liquid, discarding the vegetables. Skim off all fat from the top of the sauce. Cut the beef into ¼-inch-thick slices and return to the casserole. Pour the sauce over the meat, add the okra and simmer over low heat 5 minutes. Transfer the beef to individual plates or a platter and spoon the sauce with the okra over the slices.

Steak and Turnips

Wherever there are turnip greens, the purplish white bulb roots cannot be far away. Cooked until soft and pureed until smooth, they provide a light, low-calorie complement to juicy, pan-fried steak.

4 Servings   38% Calories from fat   225 Calories per serving

> *4 to 5 medium turnips (about 1½ pounds), peeled and quartered*
> *1 cup reduced-sodium canned chicken broth*
> *½ teaspoon salt*
> *½ teaspoon freshly ground pepper*
> *¼ teaspoon grated nutmeg*
> *Vegetable cooking spray*
> *4 well-trimmed fillet steaks, cut ¾ inch thick, about 4 ounces each*

1. In a medium saucepan, combine the turnips and the chicken broth. Add half the salt and pepper. Bring to a boil over high heat, reduce the heat to medium and cook until the turnips are very tender, about 20 minutes. Transfer to a food processor and puree until smooth. Return the pureed turnips to the saucepan and season with the nutmeg, cover and keep warm over low heat.

2. Coat a large nonstick skillet with vegetable cooking spray. Season the steaks with the remaining ¼ teaspoon each salt and pepper. Set the pan over medium-high heat, turning once, until browned outside and rare to medium-rare inside, about 4 minutes. Remove to plates or a serving platter and surround with the pureed turnips. Serve at once.

Down-Home Meat Loaf

Here's a Southern-style country crowd pleaser made lighter with ground veal and low-fat turkey. Check your supermarket meat counter to choose the leanest ground beef available. In place of fat, this savory meat loaf is kept moist with skim milk and fresh tomatoes.

8 TO 10 SERVINGS   47% CALORIES FROM FAT   202 CALORIES PER SERVING

> 2 teaspoons canola or safflower oil
> 1 small onion, finely chopped
> 3 medium tomatoes, peeled, seeded and chopped, or 1 can (16 ounces) whole peeled tomatoes, drained and chopped
> 1 pound extra-lean ground sirloin (10% fat)
> ½ pound ground veal
> ½ pound lean ground turkey
> 3 scallions (white part only), finely chopped
> ½ medium red bell pepper, finely diced
> ½ medium yellow bell pepper, finely diced
> 1 tablespoon fresh marjoram or 1 teaspoon dried
> ½ cup fresh bread crumbs
> ½ cup skim milk or water
> 1 teaspoon salt
> ½ teaspoon freshly ground pepper
> 1 egg, slightly beaten

1. In a medium nonstick saucepan, heat the oil over medium heat. Add the onion, cover and cook, stirring occasionally, until softened, about 3 minutes. Add the tomatoes, raise the heat to medium-high and cook, stirring often, until thickened, about 10 minutes. Transfer to a food processor and puree until smooth. Set the tomato sauce aside.

2. Preheat the oven to 350° F. In a large bowl, combine the ground beef, veal, turkey, scallions, red pepper, yellow pepper, marjoram, bread crumbs, milk, salt, pepper and egg. Mix until well blended.

3. Turn the meat mixture out into a nonstick roasting pan or baking dish and use damp hands to form it into an oval loaf. Pour the tomato sauce over the meat loaf and bake 1 to 1¼ hours, basting often with the sauce, until the meat loaf is cooked through and firm to the center. Serve the tomato sauce on the side.

Jacksonville Veal Lemon Roulades

Veal scallopine are just about as light and lean as meat can get. Skinless, boneless chicken breasts can be used in place of the veal, if you prefer. Serve these roulades with baked squash and turnip greens.

4 SERVINGS   28% CALORIES FROM FAT   181 CALORIES PER SERVING

> *1 pound veal scallopine, cut from the leg (8 slices)*
> *½ teaspoon salt*
> *½ teaspoon freshly ground pepper*
> *1 cup fresh bread crumbs*
> *1 tablespoon butter, melted*
> *1 tablespoon fresh lemon juice*
> *1 tablespoon chopped parsley*
> *Vegetable cooking spray*

1. Pound the veal between 2 pieces of waxed paper with a mallet or the back of a large knife until flattened to about ¼ inch thick. Season with half of the salt and pepper.

2. In a small bowl, mix together the bread crumbs, melted butter, lemon juice, parsley and remaining salt and pepper. Place 1 heaping tablespoonful of the bread crumb mixture in the center of each slice of veal and bring the opposite ends of the meat to the center, overlapping slightly to enclose the filling; secure with toothpicks.

3. Coat the bottom of a large nonstick skillet with vegetable cooking spray. Add the roulades, seam side-up, and cook over medium-high heat, turning once, until browned, about 2 minutes per side.

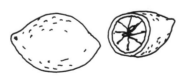

Ham with Red-Eye Gravy and Grits

This is *the* quintessential Southern breakfast, though it makes a mighty good supper, too. The "red-eye" refers to the coffee, which forms the base of the pan gravy spooned over the ham and grits. With lean and light in mind, I've used very lean ham, trimmed of all fat, and a nonstick skillet for browning.

4 SERVINGS   26% CALORIES FROM FAT   238 CALORIES PER SERVING

> *½ cup grits*
> *¼ teaspoon salt*
> *⅛ teaspoon freshly ground pepper*
> *Vegetable cooking spray*
> *1 pound lean ham steak, cut ¼ inch thick, trimmed of all fat*
> *2 tablespoons minced shallots*
> *¼ cup brewed strong black coffee*
> *½ cup reduced-sodium canned chicken broth*
> *½ teaspoon fresh thyme leaves or ¼ teaspoon dried*
> *½ teaspoon chopped fresh rosemary or ¼ teaspoon dried*

1. In a medium saucepan, bring 2½ cups of water to a boil over high heat. Stir in the grits, salt and pepper. Reduce the heat to low and cook, stirring often, 10 to 15 minutes, until all the liquid is absorbed and the grits are thickened and no longer gritty.

2. Meanwhile, coat the bottom of a large nonstick skillet with vegetable cooking spray. Heat over medium-high heat until hot but not smoking. Add the ham and cook, turning once, until lightly browned on both sides, about 5 minutes. Remove to a platter and cover with foil to keep warm.

3. Pour off any fat from the skillet. Add the shallots and cook over medium heat, stirring, until just softened, about 1 minute. Pour in the coffee, raise the heat to high and boil, scraping up any brown bits from the bottom of the pan, until reduced by half, about 1 minute. Add the chicken broth, thyme and rosemary. Boil until the sauce is again reduced by half, 2 to 3 minutes. Spoon the gravy over the ham and grits and serve at once.

Barbecued Pork Chops

While pork shoulder, or pork butt, might be used traditionally for Southern barbecue, it is too fatty in general for a health-conscious diet. This recipe uses lean, quick-cooking pork loin to deliver down-home country flavor without the fat and cholesterol.

4 SERVINGS   39% CALORIES FROM FAT   215 CALORIES PER SERVING

> ¼ *cup distilled white vinegar*
> 2 *tablespoons ketchup*
> 1 *tablespoon Worcestershire sauce*
> 1 *tablespoon prepared mustard*
> 2 *teaspoons lemon juice*
> *Several dashes of hot pepper sauce, or more to taste*
> ¼ *teaspoon salt*
> ¼ *teaspoon freshly ground pepper*
> 4 *center-cut boneless loin pork chops, trimmed of all fat, about 4 ounces each*

1. Preheat the broiler. In a small bowl, combine the vinegar, ketchup, Worcestershire sauce, mustard, lemon juice, hot sauce, salt and pepper. Stir to blend.

2. Brush the barbecue sauce evenly over both sides of the pork chops and place the chops on a broiling pan. Broil 4 to 6 inches from the heat, turning once, 8 to 10 minutes, until browned outside and white to the center but still juicy.

Sweet Potato Supper Casserole

This is a great do-ahead dish. Assemble it completely, then cover and refrigerate until you're ready to pop it in the oven. If you're adept at using a pastry bag, the sweet potato puree can be piped over the meat mixture using a decorative tip. Ground turkey can be substituted for the beef, but if you do so, add an extra ¼ cup chicken broth to keep it moist.

6 SERVINGS   37% CALORIES FROM FAT   203 CALORIES PER SERVING

> 1 tablespoon canola or safflower oil
> 1 medium onion, chopped
> 2 celery ribs, thinly sliced
> 1 garlic clove, minced
> ¾ pound lean ground beef (10% fat)
> 2 medium tomatoes, peeled, seeded and chopped
> ½ cup reduced-sodium canned chicken broth
> ¼ teaspoon salt
> ½ teaspoon pepper
> 1 tablespoon chopped fresh parsley
> 3 medium sweet potatoes, about 1 pound
> ¼ teaspoon grated nutmeg
> ½ cup orange juice

1. In a large nonstick skillet, heat the oil over medium-high heat. Add the onion and celery and cook, stirring often, until slightly softened, about 2 minutes. Add the garlic and cook 1 minute longer. Stir in the beef and cook, stirring constantly, until almost all traces of pink are gone, about 3 minutes. Stir in the tomatoes and chicken broth. Season with ¼ teaspoon each of the salt and pepper. Reduce the heat to medium and cook, stirring often, until the pan juices have thickened slightly, 5 to 7 minutes. Remove from the heat and stir in the parsley. Pour into an 8 × 11-inch baking dish and spread evenly over the bottom. Set aside.

2. Peel the sweet potatoes and cut into 1-inch pieces. Place in a large saucepan with enough cold salted water to cover by 2 inches. Bring to a boil over high heat. Reduce the heat to medium and cook until the sweet potatoes are very tender, about 10 minutes. Drain well and place in a food processor. Add the remaining ¼ teaspoon pepper, the nutmeg and the orange juice. Puree until smooth.

3. Preheat the oven to 350° F. Spoon the sweet potato puree over the meat mixture and carefully spread to cover. Bake 20 to 25 minutes, or until bubbling around the edges.

– *Pork Chops Smothered in Tomatoes and Onions* –

4 SERVINGS   39% CALORIES FROM FAT   206 CALORIES PER SERVING

> *Vegetable cooking spray*
> *4 thin-sliced center-cut boneless pork chops, trimmed of all excess fat,*
>   *about 4 ounces each*
> *1 medium onion, very thinly sliced*
> *½ cup reduced-sodium canned chicken broth*
> *2 medium tomatoes, peeled, seeded and chopped*
> *¼ teaspoon salt*
> *¼ teaspoon freshly ground pepper*
> *2 tablespoons chopped fresh parsley*

1. Coat a large nonstick skillet with vegetable cooking spray. Add the pork chops and onion and cook, turning the chops once, until the onion is softened and the meat is lightly browned, about 5 minutes. Remove to a plate and set aside.

2. Pour the chicken broth into the hot skillet. Bring to a boil, scraping up any brown bits from the bottom of the pan. Stir in the tomatoes and return the chops and onion to the skillet. Reduce the heat to medium-low and cook, partially covered, until the pork is tender, about 30 minutes.

3. Remove the chops to a platter and cover with foil to keep warm. Boil the sauce in the skillet over high heat, stirring often, until thickened, about 5 minutes. Season with the salt and pepper. Spoon the sauce over the chops, garnish with the parsley and serve at once.

Braised Pork Chops with Peaches

Fresh fruit provides a good way to lighten up most cuts of pork. The peaches here lend contrasting flavor and texture, while adding virtually no fat. Use fresh fruit that is ripe but firm. If too ripe, the cooked peaches will turn to mush.

4 SERVINGS   29% CALORIES FROM FAT   265 CALORIES PER SERVING

> 4 center-cut boneless loin pork chops, trimmed of all excess fat, about 4
>   ounces each
> ¼ teaspoon salt
> ¼ teaspoon freshly ground pepper
> Vegetable cooking spray
> 1 cup reduced-sodium canned chicken broth
> 4 large peaches, peeled, halved and pitted
> 1 tablespoon golden raisins
> 1 tablespoon chopped parsley

1. Trim the chops of any fat and season with the salt and pepper. Coat the bottom of a large nonstick skillet with vegetable cooking spray. Add the pork chops and cook over medium-high heat, turning once, until browned, about 3 minutes. Remove the chops to a plate or platter and set aside.

2. Pour the chicken broth into the skillet, raise the heat to high and boil, stirring constantly, until reduced by half, about 2 minutes. Return the pork to the skillet, reduce the heat to medium-low, cover and cook for 5 minutes. Add the peaches and raisins and continue cooking until the chops are white throughout and the peaches are tender, about 5 minutes longer.

3. Remove the chops to individual plates or a serving platter. Surround with the peaches. Boil the pan juices over high heat for 1 to 2 minutes, or until slightly thickened. Spoon over the chops and peaches, sprinkle on the parsley and serve.

Pork Chops with Apples and Bourbon

With only about 90 calories each, apples are a light fruit that adds healthy fiber, a mild sweet flavor and no fat. Golden Delicious are best for the following recipe. Granny Smith apples will do, too, providing a tart flavor that marries well with the pork and the bourbon. Greening, Mutsu, Rome Beauty, Russet or Winesap apples are good choices as well.

4 SERVINGS   32% CALORIES FROM FAT   245 CALORIES PER SERVING

> *4 center-cut boneless loin pork chops, trimmed of all excess fat, about 4 ounces each*
> *¼ teaspoon salt*
> *¼ teaspoon freshly ground pepper*
> *Vegetable cooking spray*
> *3 large cooking apples, peeled, cored and quartered*
> *½ cup bourbon*

1. Season the pork chops with the salt and pepper. Coat the bottom of a large nonstick skillet with vegetable cooking spray and heat over medium-high heat. Add the chops and cook, turning once, until browned, 3 to 5 minutes. Remove the chops to a plate and set aside.

2. Add the apples to the skillet and cook, turning gently with tongs, until lightly browned, about 5 minutes. Remove the apples to a plate.

3. Pour the bourbon into the skillet, raise the heat to high and boil until reduced by half, about 2 minutes. Return the pork chops and apples to the skillet, cover loosely and cook over medium-low heat until the chops are white throughout and tender, about 10 minutes. Remove the chops to a platter and surround with the apples.

4. Return the skillet to high heat and boil the pan juices, stirring constantly, until thick and syrupy, 1 to 2 minutes. Spoon the juices over the pork chops and apples and serve at once.

Pork Chops with Spicy Peaches

4 SERVINGS   29% CALORIES FROM FAT   269 CALORIES PER SERVING

4 center-cut pork chops with bone, cut 1 inch thick, 6 to 8 ounces each
½ teaspoon salt
¼ teaspoon freshly ground pepper
Vegetable cooking spray
1 medium onion, thinly sliced
1 cup reduced-sodium canned chicken broth
4 large peaches
½ teaspoon cinnamon
½ teaspoon grated nutmeg
2 tablespoons red wine vinegar

1. Preheat the oven to 325° F. Trim the pork chops of all fat and season with the salt and pepper. Coat the bottom of a heavy flameproof casserole with vegetable cooking spray. Heat over medium-high heat, add the chops and cook, turning, until lightly browned, about 2 minutes per side. Remove the chops and set aside.

2. Add the onion to the casserole and cook, stirring, until lightly colored, 2 to 3 minutes. Pour in the chicken broth and bring to a boil. Return the chops to the pan, cover and place in the oven. Cook 1 hour, or until the chops are very tender.

3. Meanwhile, peel the peaches and halve or quarter them. Place in a medium bowl and sprinkle on the cinnamon, nutmeg and vinegar. Gently stir to blend. Set aside at room temperature, stirring occasionally, 1 hour.

4. Remove the cooked chops to a serving platter and cover with foil to keep warm. Add the peaches with any juices in the bowl to the casserole and stir gently to coat with the pan juices. Cook over medium heat, stirring once or twice, about 3 minutes, until softened and warmed through. Spoon the peaches and any pan juices over the pork chops and serve at once.

Molasses Bourbon Glazed Pork Loin

Given modern methods of producing pork, well-trimmed loin roasts are remarkably low in fat. To keep the meat moist and prevent scorching, baste the roast frequently, adding additional water or broth as needed. Slice the roast thinly and serve with mashed sweet potatoes and collard greens.

8 SERVINGS   38% CALORIES FROM FAT   204 CALORIES PER SERVING

> *2 pounds well-trimmed center-cut boneless pork loin*
> *1/4 teaspoon salt*
> *1/4 teaspoon freshly ground pepper*
> *Vegetable cooking spray*
> *1/2 cup bourbon*
> *1/4 cup dark molasses*
> *1/4 cup reduced-sodium canned chicken broth or water*
> *1/4 teaspoon ground cloves*

1. Preheat the oven to 325° F. Be sure all excess fat has been trimmed from the meat. Season the pork with the salt and pepper. Coat the bottom of a flameproof roasting pan with vegetable cooking spray. Cook the pork over medium-high heat, turning often, until browned all over, about 5 minutes.

2. Meanwhile, in a small saucepan, combine the bourbon, molasses, broth and cloves. Heat over low heat, stirring often, until blended. Pour evenly over the pork.

3. Roast the pork in the oven, basting frequently with the pan juices, 1 hour 10 minutes, or until a meat thermometer inserted in the thickest part of the meat reaches 165° F. Remove to a carving board and let stand, loosely covered with foil, about 10 minutes before slicing.

Pork Medallions with Cabbage and Hot Pepper Sauce

A vinegary pepper sauce, sometimes known as "Pick-a-Pepper Sauce," is a clear condiment found throughout the South. It comes bottled commercially, usually with a nozzle that facilitates dispensing quick dashes of the intense liquid. To make your own, fill a jar with fresh hot peppers that have been split in half. Add a pinch of salt and fill with distilled white vinegar. Cover tightly and refrigerate for at least 2 to 3 weeks before using. Because the sauce contains no oil, it's great for zipping up flavor while keeping calories light.

4 SERVINGS   15% CALORIES FROM FAT   223 CALORIES PER SERVING

> *1 pork tenderloin, 1 to 1¼ pounds*
> *½ teaspoon salt*
> *¼ teaspoon freshly ground pepper*
> *Vegetable cooking spray*
> *½ small head of red cabbage, thinly shredded*
> *½ small head of green cabbage, thinly shredded*
> *¼ cup Pick-a-Pepper Sauce (see headnote)*
> *1 teaspoon fresh thyme leaves or ½ teaspoon dried*
> *1 tart green apple, peeled, cored and thinly sliced*

1. Trim all fat from the pork and cut the tenderloin crosswise on a slight diagonal into 8 slices about ¾ inch thick. Season these pork medallions with the salt and pepper.

2. Coat the bottom of a large nonstick skillet with vegetable cooking spray. Add the pork and cook over medium-high heat, turning once, until browned, about 4 minutes. Remove to a platter.

3. Add the red and green cabbage to the skillet. Reduce the heat to medium and cook, stirring often, until the red cabbage is wilted and the green cabbage is translucent, about 5 minutes. Stir in the pepper sauce, thyme and apple. Increase the heat to high and cook, stirring constantly, 1 minute.

4. Return the pork medallions to the skillet and reduce the heat to medium. Partially cover and cook until the pork is white throughout but still moist, 10 to 12 minutes. Arrange the pork medallions in the center of a platter and surround with the cabbage.

Pork Medallions with Mustard Greens

Mustard greens are a quintessentially Southern vegetable with a unique, pungent flavor and almost no calories. Turnip greens, collard greens or spinach can be substituted for variety. Serve with baked sweet potatoes.

4 SERVINGS   18% CALORIES FROM FAT   177 CALORIES PER SERVING

> *1 pork tenderloin, 1 to 1¼ pounds*
> *½ teaspoon salt*
> *¼ teaspoon freshly ground pepper*
> *Vegetable cooking spray*
> *1 medium shallot, minced*
> *½ cup reduced-sodium canned chicken broth*
> *1 pound mustard greens, finely shredded*

1. Trim all fat from the pork and cut the tenderloin crosswise on a slight diagonal into 8 slices about ¾ inch thick. Season the pork medallions with the salt and pepper.

2. Coat the bottom of a large nonstick skillet with vegetable cooking spray. Add the pork and cook over medium-high heat, turning once, until browned on both sides, 3 to 4 minutes. Remove to a plate.

3. Add the shallot to the skillet and cook 30 seconds. Add the chicken broth and stir to scrape up any browned bits from the bottom of the pan. Pile the greens into the skillet, pressing down to fit them in the pan. Cook over medium-high heat, stirring and pressing, until the greens have wilted down to a manageable mass, about 3 minutes.

4. Return the pork medallions to the skillet, along with any juices that have collected on the plate. Partially cover the pan and cook until the pork is white to the center with no trace of pink, 10 to 12 minutes.

5. Arrange the pork on a platter. Spoon the mustard greens around the meat, pour any pan juices over all and serve at once.

Pork Medallions with Sherry and Pecans

A light sauce is made by deglazing the pan with sherry in this recipe. This is a technique that makes the most of pan juices with no added fat. A few pecans sprinkled on top complement the nutty flavor of the sherry.

4 Servings   26% Calories from fat   207 Calories per serving

> 1 pork tenderloin, 1 to 1¼ pounds
> ¼ teaspoon salt
> ¼ teaspoon freshly ground pepper
> Vegetable cooking spray
> ½ cup dry sherry
> ¼ cup reduced-sodium canned chicken broth or water
> 1½ tablespoons chopped pecans

1. Trim off all fat from the outside of the tenderloin. Slice the meat crosswise on a slight diagonal into 8 medallions about ¾ inch thick. Season the pork with the salt and pepper. Coat the bottom of a large nonstick skillet with vegetable cooking spray. Add the pork and cook over medium-high heat, turning once, until browned, about 4 minutes. Remove to a plate.

2. Pour the sherry into the skillet. Raise the heat to high and boil, stirring constantly, until reduced by half, about 1 minute. Return the pork to the skillet and pour in the broth. Cover the pan, reduce the heat to medium-low and cook, turning the medallions once or twice, until white throughout with no trace of pink in the center, 10 to 12 minutes.

3. Remove the pork to individual plates. Boil the pan juices over high heat until thick and syrupy, about 2 minutes. Spoon the juices over the pork and sprinkle the pecans on top.

— *Pork Medallions Savannah with Tomato and* — *Garlic*

4 SERVINGS   20% CALORIES FROM FAT   159 CALORIES PER SERVING

1 pork tenderloin, 1 to 1¼ pounds
¼ teaspoon salt
¼ teaspoon freshly ground pepper
Vegetable cooking spray
2 medium tomatoes, peeled, seeded and chopped
2 garlic cloves, minced
1 tablespoon chopped fresh parsley

1. Trim all fat from the pork and cut the tenderloin crosswise on a slight diagonal into 8 slices about ¾ inch thick. Season these pork medallions with the salt and pepper.

2. Coat the bottom of a large nonstick skillet with vegetable cooking spray. Add the pork and cook over medium-high heat, turning once, until browned all over, about 4 minutes. Remove to a plate.

3. Add the tomatoes and garlic to the skillet. Bring to a boil and cook, stirring, until the garlic is slightly softened, about 1 minute. Return the pork to the skillet and reduce the heat to medium-low. Cover the pan and cook until the pork is white throughout with no trace of pink in the center, 10 to 12 minutes.

4. To serve, arrange 2 pork medallions on each of 4 plates. Stir the parsley into the tomato sauce in the skillet and spoon a small amount of sauce over each medallion.

— *Pork Tenderloin with Cherry Tomatoes and* — *Green Beans*

Healthy, light cooking stretches lean meat with plenty of fresh vegetables — here colorful cherry tomatoes and green beans, which grow year round in the South. Use small, ripe cherry tomatoes or halve larger ones. If you can find them, use half yellow tomatoes for a lovely presentation.

4 SERVINGS   18% CALORIES FROM FAT   186 CALORIES PER SERVING

1 pork tenderloin, 1 to 1¼ pounds
¼ teaspoon salt
¼ teaspoon freshly ground pepper
Vegetable cooking spray
½ cup reduced-sodium canned chicken broth or water
½ pound green beans, trimmed and cut into 1-inch pieces
35 to 40 small cherry tomatoes, about 1 pound

1. Preheat the oven to 350° F. Trim off all fat from the outside of the tenderloin. Pat the pork dry with paper towels. Season with the salt and pepper. Coat a medium flameproof casserole with vegetable cooking spray. Add the tenderloin and cook over medium-high heat, turning frequently, until lightly browned all over, about 3 minutes. Pour the chicken broth into the pan and bring to a boil. Cover and transfer the casserole to the center of the oven. Cook 20 minutes, or until the tenderloin is white to the center but still juicy.

2. Meanwhile, in a large pot of boiling salted water, cook the green beans until tender, 5 to 7 minutes. Drain and rinse under cold running water. Drain well and set aside.

3. Transfer the cooked tenderloin to a platter and cover with foil to keep warm. Place the casserole on top of the stove and bring the cooking juices to a boil over high heat. Cook, stirring constantly, until reduced by half, about 2 minutes. Add the cherry tomatoes and green beans to the casserole and stir over high heat until the tomatoes are slightly softened and the beans are heated through, about 3 minutes.

4. To serve, carve the tenderloin crosswise on a slight diagonal into 8 thick slices. Surround the pork with the vegetables.

Chapter Five

FISH
AND
SHELLFISH

When I was growing up in Georgia, there was a big community fish fry every year. I have vivid memories of huge black skillets full of bubbling lard that held many morsels of golden brown catfish fillets. As fond as those recollections are, in today's health-conscious kitchen, a pan of lard will never look the same. Luckily, we've learned that fish doesn't have to be deep-fried to be good and that there are excellent alternatives to saturated fats.

Low in saturated fat, high in protein, full of vitamins and minerals and generally low in sodium, fish is a natural part of a healthful menu. Using an assortment of traditional Southern ingredients, this chapter bakes, broils and steams fish to provide tasty low-fat dishes even the Colonel would approve of. Baked Catfish with Red and Yellow Peppers, Bluefish en Papillote, Lemon and Lime Baked Red Snapper, Grilled Kingfish with White Wine and Lime and Scalloped Oysters are just a few of the recipes that combine low-calorie cooking with Southern flavor.

Living in the South often means living close to water. The Atlantic coast and the Gulf of Mexico plus an endless array of winding rivers, lakes, backwaters and waterways provide this part of the world with lots of fish. The Chesapeake Bay is home to crabs and bluefish, so popular in Virginia, Maryland and North Carolina. Porgy and Bess, one of America's favorite stories, recounts the life of selling fish on the streets of

Charleston, where she-crabs and shrimp have long been a part of every-day living. Savannah in coastal Georgia is home to a thriving fishing industry as is Jacksonville on the northern Florida Atlantic coastline. The Gulf of Mexico provides much of the South with a plethora of fish and shellfish as do the Mississippi Delta region, the bayous of Louisiana and the Galveston Bay. Inland rivers and lakes provide freshwater species of trout, bass and catfish.

When buying fish, look for gleaming, firm flesh and bright eyes. The flesh should spring back slightly and not be mushy when pressed lightly with a finger. The fish should smell clean, oceanlike and delicate. Scales should be tight and shiny. If there are gills, they should be vibrantly bright red. Fish fillets and steaks should be firm, moist and translucent, not dry, listless or discolored around the edges. Avoid cut fish that sits in trays of excess liquid. Shrimp should be firm, not mushy and limp. Oysters should be tightly closed but alive. Crabs should be kept in clean, deep tanks. Choose with care, trust your fishmonger and demand the best.

Lemon-Broiled Bluefish with Fresh Tomato Relish

Bluefish is a good fish for broiling. A simple preparation like the following is my flavorite way to cook this somewhat oily fish. Serve with your favorite bottled or homemade salsa.

4 SERVINGS   37% CALORIES FROM FAT   250 CALORIES PER SERVING

2 medium tomatoes, cored and chopped
2 tablespoons red wine vinegar
2 tablespoons chopped fresh parsley
Vegetable cooking spray
2 teaspoons canola oil
4 bluefish fillets, about 6 ounces each
2 tablespoons fresh lemon juice
1/2 teaspoon salt
1/4 teaspoon freshly ground pepper
1/4 teaspoon paprika

1. In a small bowl, combine the tomatoes, vinegar and parsley. Cover and set the tomato relish aside at room temperature for 1 hour to allow the flavors to develop.

2. Preheat the broiler. Coat a broiling pan with vegetable cooking spray and brush about 1/2 teaspoon of oil over each fillet. Sprinkle each with 1/2 tablespoon lemon juice and season with the salt and pepper.

3. Broil 4 to 6 inches from the heat 8 to 10 minutes, or until the top is lightly browned and the fish is opaque throughout. Remove from the oven, dust with the paprika and serve at once, with the room-temperature tomato relish on the side.

Poached Striped Bass with Cajun Remoulade Sauce

The Chesapeake Bay is home to a number of striped bass. A popular fish in Virginia and the Carolinas, the bass has a sweet, succulent flesh that lends itself to poaching. The Cajun Remoulade Sauce adds a little punch that most Southerners appreciate. A fish poacher is handy for this recipe. If not available, use a roasting pan large enough to hold the fish flat. Wrap it in cheesecloth to facilitate lifting the cooked fish to a platter. Garnish the platter with lemon slices, cherry tomatoes and lots of parsley sprigs or fresh dill.

4 TO 6 SERVINGS   23% CALORIES FROM FAT   211 CALORIES PER SERVING

1 bottle (750 ml) dry white wine
1 celery rib, thickly sliced
2 medium carrots, peeled and coarsely chopped
1 medium onion, coarsely chopped
Several sprigs of fresh thyme or 1 teaspoon dried thyme leaves
Several sprigs of parsley
1 bay leaf
¼ teaspoon salt
10 whole black peppercorns
1 whole striped bass, 5 to 6 pounds, cleaned and scaled, head and tail intact
Cajun Remoulade Sauce (recipe follows)

1. Combine 6 cups of water, the wine, celery, carrots, onion, thyme, parsley, bay leaf, salt and peppercorns in a large nonreactive saucepan. Bring to a boil over high heat. Reduce the heat to medium-high and cook, partially covered, for 30 minutes. Strain the liquid and discard the solids.

2. Preheat the oven to 350° F. Place the fish in a fish poacher or in a large roasting pan. Pour over the strained liquid. (Add additional water if necessary to completely cover the fish.) Bring to a simmer on top of the stove and carefully transfer to the oven. Cover with a lid or foil. Poach gently until the fish is firm to the touch and opaque throughout, about 30 minutes. An instant-reading thermometer inserted in the thickest point should read 140° F.

3. Remove the fish to a serving platter and cover loosely with foil. Let stand for 20 minutes. Carefully peel away the skin and garnish as desired. Serve with the sauce on the side.

Cajun Remoulade Sauce

MAKES ABOUT 1 CUP   87% CALORIES FROM FAT   42 CALORIES PER TABLESPOON

1 cup low-fat mayonnaise
1 small shallot, minced
1 tablespoon chopped chives
1 tablespoon chopped parsley
1 tablespoon chopped chervil
1 tablespoon capers, chopped
1 teaspoon Dijon mustard
1/2 teaspoon salt
1/4 teaspoon freshly ground pepper

Combine the mayonnaise, shallot, chives, parsley, chervil, mustard and capers in a small bowl. Stir to blend well. Season with the salt and pepper. Cover and refrigerate until ready to serve.

Bluefish en Papillote

A friend of mine from Virginia swears that bluefish is the only species of fish he'll eat besides fish sticks. That's how common they are in many coastal areas of the South. Cooking fish in foil or paper seals in juices and allows cooking with virtually no fat. Try substituting a couple of tablespoons of lemon juice if tomatoes are not in season.

4 Servings   30% Calories from fat   227 Calories per serving

    4 bluefish fillets, about 6 ounces each
    5 ounces medium mushrooms, thinly sliced
    1 large ripe tomato, peeled, seeded and chopped
    1 teaspoon fresh thyme leaves or ½ teaspoon dried
    ¼ teaspoon salt
    ¼ teaspoon freshly ground pepper

1. Preheat the oven to 425° F. Place the fish on the short ends of 4 pieces of parchment paper or aluminum foil that measure 12 inches wide by 15 inches long. Top each with several slices of mushroom and equal amounts of chopped tomato. Season with the thyme, salt and pepper. Fold over the opposite short end and crimp the edges all around to form a tight seal.

2. Place the fish packages on 1 or 2 large baking sheets and bake 12 to 15 minutes, or until puffed. Serve in the paper or remove the fillets to plates and spoon the mushrooms, tomatoes and juices over the fish.

Baked Catfish with Mushrooms and White Wine

Catfish are a staple of Southern cooking. While they used to be a treat carried home on the end of a fishing line, Mississippi entrepreneurs have discovered that farm-raising catfish is a lucrative enterprise. It was a surprise to me to learn that probably because of their diet, these cultivated fish are lighter and leaner than their wild cousins. White, lean fillets are distributed throughout the country these days and inventive cooks are learning just how versatile catfish can be.

4 SERVINGS   49% CALORIES FROM FAT   310 CALORIES PER SERVING

1 tablespoon canola or safflower oil
¾ pound mushrooms, thinly sliced
1 garlic clove, minced
½ cup dry white wine
3 medium tomatoes, peeled, seeded and chopped
½ teaspoon salt
¼ teaspoon freshly ground pepper
4 catfish fillets, about 6 ounces each

1. Preheat the oven to 425° F. Heat the oil in a large nonstick skillet over medium-high heat. Add the mushrooms and garlic. Cook, stirring occasionally, until the mushrooms are lightly browned, about 3 minutes.

2. Pour in the wine, increase the heat to high and boil until reduced by half. Add the tomatoes, salt and pepper. Bring to a boil and cook, stirring occasionally, until the sauce is slightly thickened, about 3 minutes.

3. Arrange the catfish fillets in a baking dish large enough to hold them flat. Pour the mushrooms and sauce over the fish. Cover the dish tightly with aluminum foil and bake 12 to 15 minutes, or until the fish is firm and opaque throughout.

Oven-Fried Catfish

Catfish can be "fried" in the oven with surprisingly good results. While nothing can replace the flavor of frying in deep fat, this lightened-up version of the real thing is a healthier alternative. Stale cornbread, worked through a fine-mesh sieve, can be used in place of bread crumbs. Serve with coleslaw and hushpuppies.

6 SERVINGS   47% CALORIES FROM FAT   303 CALORIES PER SERVING

> *Vegetable cooking spray*
> *1 cup dry bread crumbs*
> *½ cup skim milk*
> *2 pounds catfish fillets*
> *½ teaspoon salt*
> *¼ teaspoon freshly ground pepper*
> *2 tablespoons butter, melted*

1. Preheat the oven to 475° F. Coat a baking dish large enough to hold the fish in a single layer with vegetable cooking spray.

2. Place the bread crumbs on a large sheet of wax paper. Pour the milk into a shallow dish. Season the fish with the salt and pepper. Dip in the milk and let any excess drain off. Roll in the bread crumbs to coat and transfer to the baking dish.

3. Drizzle the butter over the fish and bake 7 to 10 minutes, until well browned and opaque throughout.

Herbed Catfish

Catfish is a mild-flavored fish that takes well to seasonings. Fresh herbs make all the difference in this recipe. The amount and kinds can be varied but the mint adds a truly Southern flavor. Rosemary can be substituted for the thyme, fresh oregano can take the place of parsley and if you're lucky enough to have some lemon thyme, you'll find that it adds a lovely subtle flavor that marries well with the mint. Serve with lemon wedges and steamed spinach.

4 Servings   50% Calories from fat   241 Calories per serving

> ½ *small onion, minced*
> 4 *catfish fillets, about 6 ounces each*
> ¼ *teaspoon salt*
> ¼ *teaspoon freshly ground pepper*
> 1 *tablespoon chopped fresh parsley*
> 2 *teaspoons chopped fresh thyme or* ½ *teaspoon dried*
> 2 *teaspoons chopped fresh mint or* ½ *teaspoon dried*
> ½ *cup dry white wine*

1. Preheat the oven to 425° F. Sprinkle the onion over the bottom of a baking dish large enough to hold the catfish in a single layer. Arrange the fillets in the dish and season with the salt and pepper. Sprinkle the parsley, thyme and mint over the catfish and pour the wine into the dish.

2. Cover tightly with foil and bake 12 to 15 minutes, until the fish is opaque throughout.

Baked Catfish with Red and Yellow Peppers

This is a lean, colorful way to prepare that old-time favorite Southern fish. I often add a touch of cumin to the peppers while they cook for an exotic touch. Serve with rice and green beans.

4 SERVINGS   53% CALORIES FROM FAT   287 CALORIES PER SERVING

1 tablespoon canola or safflower oil
1 medium red bell pepper, thinly sliced
1 medium yellow bell pepper, thinly sliced
1 medium onion, thinly sliced
1 garlic clove, minced
½ cup dry white wine
4 catfish fillets, 6 ounces each
½ teaspoon ground cumin
½ teaspoon salt
¼ teaspoon freshly ground pepper
1 tablespoon chopped parsley

1. Preheat the oven to 425° F. In a large nonstick skillet, heat the oil over medium-high heat. Add the red pepper, yellow pepper, onion and garlic. Reduce the heat to medium-low, cover and cook, stirring often, until softened, about 5 minutes. Remove from the heat and pour in the wine.

2. Arrange the catfish fillets flat in an 8 × 11-inch baking dish. Season with the cumin, salt and pepper. Pour the pepper and wine mixture over the fish and cover the dish with aluminum foil.

3. Bake 10 to 12 minutes, or until the fish is firm and white throughout. Transfer the fillets to a large serving platter. Surround with the peppers. Drizzle any pan juices over the fish, garnish with the parsley and serve at once.

— *Steamed Catfish with Tomato Mint Sauce* —

4 SERVINGS   53% CALORIES FROM FAT   265 CALORIES PER SERVING

1 ripe tomato, cored and cut into ¼-inch dice
½ red onion, thinly sliced
1 tablespoon chopped fresh mint or 1 teaspoon dried
1 tablespoon canola or safflower oil
2 tablespoons fresh lime juice
½ teaspoon salt
½ teaspoon freshly ground pepper
4 catfish fillets, 6 ounces each

1. In a medium bowl, combine the tomato, onion, mint, oil, lime juice and half of the salt and pepper. Stir to blend, cover and leave at room temperature for 1 hour.

2. Season the fillets with the remaining ¼ teaspoon salt and ¼ teaspoon pepper. In a large saucepan fitted with a steamer rack or in a Chinese steamer, cook the fish over medium-high heat until firm and opaque throughout, 7 to 10 minutes. Transfer to serving plates and serve hot.

— *Crab Cakes* —

These cakes are baked rather than browned in fat. The color will not be the same, but the flavor is just as good. Serve with a squeeze of lemon or a tartar sauce made with reduced-calorie mayonnaise.

4 SERVINGS   31% CALORIES FROM FAT   370 CALORIES PER SERVING

1 tablespoon butter
1 medium onion, finely chopped
1 celery rib, finely chopped
½ garlic clove, minced
1 pound fresh lump crabmeat
1 cup fresh bread crumbs
1 tablespoon chopped parsley
1 teaspoon grated lemon zest
1 tablespoon lemon juice
½ teaspoon salt
¼ teaspoon freshly ground pepper
1 cup cornmeal
Vegetable cooking spray

1. Preheat the oven to 425° F. Melt the butter in a medium nonstick skillet. Add the onion, celery and garlic and stir to coat. Cover and cook over medium heat 2 minutes. Uncover and continue to cook, stirring occasionally, until softened but not brown, about 2 minutes longer.

2. In a medium bowl, combine the crabmeat, bread crumbs, parsley, lemon zest, lemon juice, salt and pepper with the cooked onion, celery and garlic. Stir gently to blend. Using wet hands, form into 8 small cakes about 2 inches in diameter. Place the cornmeal in a shallow bowl and dredge each crab cake in cornmeal to coat; shake off any excess.

3. Spray a nonstick baking sheet with vegetable cooking spray. Arrange the cakes on the sheet and bake, turning once, for 12 to 15 minutes, or until browned.

Deviled Crab

In some stores throughout the South, empty crab shells for making this dish are available for sale. The dish is just as tasty when prepared in small ramekins, even if the look isn't quite the same. Serve these as a first course with lemon wedges.

6 SERVINGS   41% CALORIES FROM FAT   174 CALORIES PER SERVING

> 1 pound crabmeat
> 2 egg whites
> 1½ cups fresh bread crumbs
> 1 tablespoon fresh lemon juice
> 1 teaspoon Dijon mustard
> ½ teaspoon salt
> 1 tablespoon Worcestershire sauce
> Several drops of hot pepper sauce, or more to taste
> ⅓ cup reduced-calorie mayonnaise
> Vegetable cooking spray
> 1 tablespoon butter, melted
> Paprika, for dusting

1. Preheat the oven to 400° F. In a small bowl, combine the crabmeat, egg whites, bread crumbs, lemon juice, mustard, salt, Worcestershire sauce, hot sauce and mayonnaise. Blend well.

2. Spray 6 small (½-cup capacity) ramekins with vegetable cooking spray. Divide the crab mixture among the ramekins, drizzle ½ teaspoon of melted butter over each and dust lightly with paprika.

3. Bake 15 minutes, or until lightly browned on top and bubbly.

Crawfish Boil

There is no delicacy quite like crawfish. These lobsterlike crustaceans are best known in Louisiana but are increasingly found throughout the country. Smart entrepreneurs have found crawfish easy to farm and even easier to market. South Carolina, for example, boasts a large industry devoted to this sort of aquaculture.

For a festive, informal party, do as we Southerners do—spread newspapers over the table and let guests peel their own right out of the bowl. Use a low-fat Italian salad dressing for dipping in place of the traditional drawn butter. Serve with corn on the cob and coleslaw.

4 SERVINGS   11% CALORIES FROM FAT   97 CALORIES PER SERVING

8 pounds live crawfish
1 tablespoon salt
2 lemons, halved
1 medium onion, halved
2 garlic cloves, coarsely chopped
2 teaspoons crushed hot red pepper
1 teaspoon dried thyme leaves
10 black peppercorns
2 bay leaves

1. Place the crawfish in a large bowl and cover with cold water. Rinse well and discard those that show no signs of life.

2. In a large stockpot or soup kettle, combine the salt, lemons, onion and garlic. In a small piece of cheesecloth, tie together the hot pepper, thyme, peppercorns and bay leaves. Add to the pot along with 2 gallons of water. Bring to a boil over high heat. Boil rapidly for 15 minutes. Remove and discard the spice bag.

3. Add the crawfish to the pot, return to a boil and cook until firm and bright red, 7 to 10 minutes. Drain and serve at once.

Grilled Kingfish with White Wine and Lime

Kingfish is the common Southern name for king mackerel, a large member of this dark-fleshed family of fish, which is found all along the Carolina coast on into Florida and down into the Caribbean. Rich in omega-3 oils, high in protein and low in calories, this fish has long been a favorite with Southerners. Fresh tuna or swordfish are the closest substitutes.

4 Servings   27% Calories from fat   210 Calories per serving

1½ pounds kingfish fillets, cut into 4 equal pieces
3 tablespoons dry white wine
2 tablespoons fresh lime juice
1 tablespoon canola or safflower oil
½ small onion, finely chopped
1 teaspoon fresh thyme leaves or ½ teaspoon dried
¼ teaspoon salt
⅛ teaspoon freshly ground pepper

1. Place the kingfish fillets in a single layer in a nonreactive baking dish just large enough to hold them in a single layer. In a small bowl, combine the wine, lime juice, oil, onion, thyme, salt and pepper. Stir to mix well. Pour the marinade over the fish, cover and refrigerate, turning often, 2 to 3 hours.

2. Meanwhile, prepare a hot fire in a charcoal grill and allow the coals to burn down to a gray ash. Remove the fish from the marinade and pat dry with paper towels. Grill about 4 inches from the heat, turning once and basting often with the marinade, until lightly browned and opaque throughout, 8 to 10 minutes. Note: Stop basting the fish about 2 minutes before it is done so that the marinade has a chance to cook.

Mustard Broiled Mullet

The panhandle of Florida, with its long white beaches, is a lovely part of the world. All along the Gulf Coast that surrounds the panhandle, from Alabama to Louisiana and Texas, mullet seems to be as much a part of the scenery as the low-hanging moss that abounds down there. Substitute mackerel or bluefish for a similar taste.

4 SERVINGS   32% CALORIES FROM FAT   211 CALORIES PER SERVING

Vegetable cooking spray
2½ tablespoons Dijon mustard
4 mullet fillets, about 6 ounces each
1½ teaspoons lemon juice
¼ teaspoon salt
¼ teaspoon freshly ground pepper
¼ teaspoon paprika

1. Preheat the broiler. Coat a broiling pan with vegetable cooking spray and brush about ½ tablespoon of mustard over each fillet. Sprinkle on the lemon juice and season with the salt and pepper.

2. Broil 4 to 6 inches from the heat 8 to 10 minutes, or until the top is lightly brown and the fish is opaque throughout. Remove from the oven, dust with the paprika and serve at once.

Scalloped Oysters

My cousin, Anna, was often in charge of Thanksgiving. She came from Dothan, Alabama, which is not far from Apalachicola, Florida. This Gulf Coast town is known for its big, tasty oysters, which most folks down South like to dip in cornmeal and fry like doughnuts. They also love them scalloped. Anna always had scalloped oysters alongside her turkey and dressing. I've lightened up her version with a fat-free cracker crumb that is new on the market and by using skim milk and cutting the butter. Honestly, the dish is just as tasty as I remember it being all those years ago. Buy the oysters already shucked to save a lot of time and trouble.

6 SERVINGS   25% CALORIES FROM FAT   336 CALORIES PER SERVING

> *Vegetable cooking spray*
> *1 quart shucked oysters*
> *1/2 teaspoon salt*
> *1/4 teaspoon freshly ground pepper*
> *2 tablespoons butter, cut into thin slivers*
> *2 cups packaged fat-free cracker crumbs*
> *1/2 cup skim milk*
> *1 egg*
> *1/2 cup dry bread crumbs*

1. Coat the bottom of a 9 × 13-inch baking dish with vegetable cooking spray. Layer the bottom with one-third of the oysters. Season with one-third of the salt and pepper. Dot with slivers of butter. Sprinkle over one-third of the cracker crumbs. Continue with the remaining oysters and crackers, seasoning with salt and pepper and dotting with butter.

2. Preheat the oven to 350° F. In a small bowl, beat together the milk and the egg. Pour over the oysters and crackers. Top with the bread crumbs and bake until the oysters are cooked through and the crumbs are lightly browned on top, about 30 minutes. Serve at once.

Pompano en Papillote

Pompano is a delicacy well known throughout the South. It is native to the Eastern seaboard from North Carolina to Florida. It has a delicate, sweet flesh that lends itself to simple preparations. Cooking in foil is great for light fare. The small amount of butter adds flavor but virtually no other fat is needed to insure a moist, succulent success. Because the steam is held in, moisture permeates the fish and prevents any chance of drying out. Serve with boiled potatoes and a fresh green vegetable like broccoli or something leafy like spinach.

4 SERVINGS   55% CALORIES FROM FAT   157 CALORIES PER SERVING

4 pompano fillets, about 6 ounces each
1/4 pound medium shrimp, shelled and deveined
4 teaspoons butter, cut into slivers
1/4 cup dry white wine
1/2 cup thinly shredded basil
1/2 teaspoon salt
1/4 teaspoon freshly ground pepper

1. Preheat the oven to 425° F. Arrange the pompano in the center of 4 pieces of foil that measure 12 inches wide and 15 inches long. Finely chop the shrimp and divide among the fillets. Dot with slivers of butter, spoon 1 tablespoon of the wine over each and scatter over the basil. Season with the salt and pepper. Fold the top of the foil over the bottom and crimp the edges to seal tightly.

2. Place on a baking sheet and bake until puffed and the fish is cooked through, about 10 minutes.

Salmon Croquettes

As a transplanted Georgia boy living in New York, I used to frequent a restaurant in Greenwich Village called The Pink Tea Cup, a dressed-up coffee shop specializing in true Southern cuisine. On Sunday mornings, my favorite brunch was their salmon croquettes with grits and scrambled eggs. A wave of nostalgia would just about knock me off the wobbly stool when the plate arrived. The Pink Tea Cup has moved and improved since then and my salmon croquettes are baked instead of fried.

6 SERVINGS   31% CALORIES FROM FAT   217 CALORIES PER SERVING

2 tablespoons butter
2 tablespoons all-purpose flour
1/2 cup skim milk
2 teaspoons lemon juice
1/4 teaspoon salt
1/8 teaspoon cayenne pepper
1 can (14 3/4 ounces) salmon, bones removed
1 cup yellow cornmeal

1. In a small saucepan, melt the butter over medium-high heat. Add the flour and stir to blend. Cook, stirring constantly, for 1 minute. Pour in the milk and bring to a boil. Reduce the heat to medium and cook, stirring often, until thickened, 5 to 10 minutes. Remove from the heat and season with the lemon juice, salt and cayenne. Let cool to room temperature.

2. Flake the salmon in a large bowl. Pour in the white sauce and beat with a wooden spoon until the mixture is stiff. Use your hands to form it into 12 oval croquettes about 2 inches in diameter.

3. Preheat the oven to 425° F. Roll the croquettes in the cornmeal to coat. Place them on a nonstick baking sheet and bake for 15 minutes, turning once, or until lightly browned.

Barbecued Shrimp

Barbecued anything is a popular Southern tradition. These shrimp are a testament to the talent that Southerners have for this kind of simple cooking. Serve with rice and a "mess" of greens.

4 SERVINGS   29% CALORIES FROM FAT   123 CALORIES PER SERVING

> *2 tablespoons light soy sauce*
> *2 tablespoons ketchup*
> *2 tablespoons canola or safflower oil*
> *1 tablespoon lemon juice*
> *1 garlic clove, minced*
> *¼ teaspoon cayenne pepper*
> *24 large shrimp (about 1 pound), shelled and deveined*

1. In a small bowl, combine the soy sauce, ketchup, oil, lemon juice, garlic and cayenne pepper. Stir to blend well. Place the shrimp in a nonreactive baking dish and pour the sauce over them; turn to coat. Cover and refrigerate, stirring and turning often, at least 2 hours.

2. Preheat the broiler or light a charcoal fire and allow the coals to burn down to a gray ash. Using 8 long metal skewers, thread 3 shrimp through the head and tail onto each one. Broil or grill 4 to 6 inches from the heat, brushing frequently with the marinade and turning once, until the shrimp are bright pink and curled, 2 to 3 minutes on each side.

Shrimp Creole

6 SERVINGS   29% CALORIES FROM FAT   257 CALORIES PER SERVING

> 3 tablespoons canola or safflower oil
> 1 small onion, finely chopped
> 1 celery rib, finely chopped
> ½ green bell pepper, finely chopped
> 1 garlic clove, minced
> 3 medium tomatoes, peeled, seeded and chopped, or 1 can (14 ounces)
>   tomatoes, drained
> ½ teaspoon salt
> ¼ teaspoon cayenne pepper
> 1 teaspoon filé gumbo (optional)
> 1 cup long-grain white rice
> 1 pound medium shrimp, shelled and deveined

1. In a medium skillet, melt 2 tablespoons of the oil over moderate heat. Add the onion, celery, green pepper and garlic. Cook, stirring often, until softened, about 2 minutes. Stir in the tomatoes and add ¼ teaspoon of the salt, the cayenne pepper and the filé gumbo. Increase the heat to high and boil until the sauce is slightly thickened, 5 to 10 minutes. Set aside.

2. In a small covered saucepan, pour in the remaining tablespoon of oil. Add the rice and cook over moderately high heat, stirring constantly, until translucent, 1 to 2 minutes. Bring 2 cups of water to a boil and pour over the rice. Bring back to a boil, immediately reduce the heat to low, add the remaining ¼ teaspoon salt, cover and cook for 20 minutes. Remove the cover, stir gently with a fork, cover again and let sit off heat for 5 minutes.

3. Meanwhile, add the shrimp to the tomato sauce mixture. Bring to a boil and stir until the shrimp turn pink and are firm to the touch, 3 to 5 minutes.

4. Arrange the rice on a serving platter. Spoon over the Shrimp Creole and serve at once.

Curried Shrimp

In my Georgia home, curried shrimp was often the main course served when company came for dinner, which was often the noonday meal on weekends. While the curry itself was simple, a large assortment of condiments were offered on the side to dress it up.

4 Servings   23% Calories from fat   321 Calories per serving

> 2 tablespoons butter
> ½ small onion, finely chopped
> 1 tablespoon flour
> 2 teaspoons curry powder
> 1 medium tomato, peeled, seeded and chopped
> 1 cup skim milk
> 1 pound medium shrimp, shelled and deveined
> 2 cups hot, cooked long-grain white rice
>
> Optional garnishes:
> Chopped dry-roasted peanuts—18 calories per teaspoon
> Crumbled cooked lean bacon—14 calories per teaspoon
> Chopped onion—1 calorie per teaspoon
> Chopped hard-cooked egg—4 calories per teaspoon
> Mango chutney—16 calories per teaspoon

1. In a small saucepan, melt the butter over medium-high heat. Add the onion and cook, stirring often, until softened, about 2 minutes. Stir in the flour and curry powder and cook, stirring, 1 minute longer. Add the tomato, stir well to blend and cook 2 minutes longer.

2. Pour in the milk and bring to a boil, whisking until smooth and thickened, 1 to 2 minutes. Lower the heat to medium-low and simmer, stirring or whisking often, 3 minutes longer.

3. Add the shrimp to the sauce, partially cover and cook, stirring often, until the shrimp are pink and curled, about 3 minutes. Serve over the rice, with bowls of the garnishes on the side.

Shrimp Salad with Peanuts

Roasted peanuts add crunch and flavor to this shrimp salad. Serve as a first course or on a buffet with several other cold dishes.

4 Servings   44% Calories from fat   209 Calories per serving

1 pound medium shrimp, peeled and deveined
1 tablespoon fresh lemon or lime juice
¼ cup nonfat plain yogurt
¼ cup reduced-calorie mayonnaise
1 medium red bell pepper, diced
1 celery rib, thinly sliced
2 scallions, thinly sliced
¼ cup roasted peanuts, coarsely chopped
1 tablespoon chopped fresh parsley
½ teaspoon salt
¼ teaspoon freshly ground pepper

1. Bring 3 cups water to a boil in a large saucepan over high heat. Add the shrimp and cook until bright pink, 3 to 5 minutes. Drain and rinse under cold water to stop the cooking. Drain on paper towels for 10 or 15 minutes, then transfer to a bowl and refrigerate until well chilled.

2. In a medium bowl, combine the lemon juice, yogurt and mayonnaise. Stir until blended. Pour over the shrimp. Add the red pepper, celery, scallions, peanuts and parsley. Stir to coat well. Season with the salt and pepper, cover and refrigerate for about 1 hour, or until well chilled.

Lemon and Lime Baked Red Snapper

Red snapper makes its way to Georgia, the Carolinas and Virginia from the warmer waters of Florida and the Gulf of Mexico. The lemon and lime add a pleasing acidic flavor, which marries well with the sweetness of the snapper. Slice the fruits as thin as possible so that they soften in the short amount of time it takes to cook the fish. Present the snapper whole on a platter surrounded with the cooked lemon and lime slices as garnish. Serve with broiled tomatoes and boiled potatoes.

Seafood
126

4 Servings   13% Calories from fat   195 Calories per serving

Vegetable cooking spray
½ small lemon, sliced paper thin
½ small lime, sliced paper thin
1 whole red snapper, about 3 pounds, scaled and cleaned, head and tail
*   intact*
2 sprigs of fresh thyme or ¼ teaspoon dried leaves
1 garlic clove, minced
¼ teaspoon salt
¼ teaspoon freshly ground pepper
¼ cup dry white wine or water

1. Preheat the oven to 450° F. Coat the bottom of a baking dish large enough to hold the fish flat with vegetable cooking spray. Scatter the lemon and lime slices over the bottom of the dish and lay the fish on top of them. Place the thyme sprigs in the cavity of the snapper or season with the dried thyme. Sprinkle the garlic over the top of the fish and season with the salt and pepper.

2. Pour the wine into the bottom of the baking dish. Cover loosely with foil and bake, basting the fish once or twice with the pan juices, 20 to 25 minutes, or until the fish is opaque near the bone.

VEGETABLES
AND
SIDE
DISHES

We are blessed with a long, warm growing season in the South. Beans, peas, tomatoes, peppers, onions, corn, squash, okra and sweet potatoes thrive in the moist lushness of green fields and fertile river banks. Nature has given us a bounty unequaled in other parts of the country.

And what a wonderful way to enjoy lighter, more nutritious cooking! Fresh vegetables are satisfying, nutritious and low in fats and calories and they contain no cholesterol. They can be enhanced with the simplest treatments. Rather than adding bacon, ham hocks or salt pork and cooking vegetables for hours as was once the custom, the updated recipes that follow call for relatively quick cooking times with only nonfattening ingredients like lemon, vinegar, peppers, broth and tomatoes for embellishment.

Collard greens, mustard greens and turnip greens are old Southern vegetables that are increasingly popular throughout the country and often available at local farmers' markets. Many farmers find them easy to grow, and they are inexpensive. That's good news for consumers who want a low-calorie, intensely flavorful vegetable with lots of fiber. In addition, these greens are high in calcium, iron and vitamin A. Tangy Collard Greens with Sweet Red Peppers, Creamed Collards and Stewed Mustard Greens present quick-cooking, healthy ways to treat these Southern favorites.

Classic side dishes made from grains and beans, such as grits, fritters and Hoppin' John, are included in this chapter, too. Grits are derived from hominy, a corn product treated to remove the tough outer layers, then boiled, dried and ground into a cereal that can be cooked like porridge. It is traditionally served for breakfast, seasoned only with butter, salt and pepper. We've included a variety of recipes that use grits as a side dish. Baked Grits with Onions and Tomato Sauce, Texas Cheese Grits and Oven-Browned Grits with Parsley and Chives take this Southern staple to a new plateau. Cooked with skim milk and a minimum amount of eggs and butter, these light dishes are the perfect accompaniment for grilled meats or chicken.

When planning a Southern menu, vegetables are a primary consideration. Choose the freshest and best of what's in season. Plan to use contrasting colors and textures that complement each other like tomatoes and corn, greens and squash or sweet potatoes and green beans. Serve vegetables balanced with a minimum amount of lean meat, poultry or fish for a traditional meal that won't tip the scales.

Tangy Collard Greens with Sweet Red Peppers

Blanching the greens—that is, precooking them quickly in boiling water—reduces the amount of time needed to break down the tough fibers. Rather than stewing the collards for hours the old-fashioned way with a piece of ham hock, bacon or salt pork, this light version sautés them for a relatively short time with peppers, onion and a splash of vinegar. The result is a fresh, clean taste with plenty of vibrant color. Serve with any grilled meat or chicken.

4 Servings   36% Calories from fat   86 Calories per serving

> 2 pounds collard greens
> 1 tablespoon canola or safflower oil
> 1 large red bell pepper
> 1 medium onion, thinly sliced
> 2 tablespoons red wine vinegar
> 1/4 teaspoon salt
> 1/8 teaspoon freshly ground pepper

1. Tear the tough stems off the bottoms of the collard greens. Rinse the greens well in several changes of cold water to remove any grit.

2. Bring a large pot of salted water to a boil. Add the collard greens and return the water to a boil. Cook over high heat 5 minutes. Drain and rinse under cold running water; drain well. Squeeze the greens gently to remove as much liquid as possible. Coarsely chop the collard greens.

3. In a large nonstick skillet, heat the oil over medium heat. Add the bell pepper and onion and cook, stirring often, until softened, about 3 minutes. Pour in the vinegar and raise the heat to high. Cook, stirring, until the vinegar is almost evaporated, about 1 minute.

4. Add the chopped collard greens to the skillet and season with the salt and pepper. Cook over medium-high heat, stirring, until warmed through, about 2 minutes. Serve hot.

Creamed Collards

A small amount of cream is all that is needed to bind the collards into a puree that makes a delicious side dish. Serve with meat loaf and yellow squash for a light but satisfying meal.

4 SERVINGS   26% CALORIES FROM FAT   97 CALORIES PER SERVING

> *2 pounds collard greens, tough stems removed*
> *1 teaspoon fresh lemon juice*
> *2 tablespoons heavy cream*
> *¼ teaspoon salt*
> *¼ teaspoon freshly ground pepper*

1. In a large saucepan of boiling salted water, cook the collard greens until tender, about 2 minutes. Drain and rinse under cold running water. Drain well.

2. In a food processor, puree the collards with the lemon juice. Transfer to a medium saucepan and add the cream, salt and pepper. Cook the collards over medium heat, stirring often, until warmed through, about 2 minutes. Serve hot.

Corn Fritters

This down-home treat is lightened up by using skim milk in the batter and cooking the fritters with vegetable cooking spray instead of bacon fat. The results are surprisingly good. Try them with grilled chicken or lean roast beef.

6 SERVINGS   24% CALORIES FROM FAT   87 CALORIES PER SERVING

> *2 eggs*
> *2 tablespoons skim milk*
> *½ teaspoon salt*
> *¼ teaspoon freshly ground pepper*
> *2 cups fresh corn kernels or 1 package (10 ounces) frozen corn, thawed*

3 tablespoons flour
1 teaspoon baking powder
Vegetable cooking spray

1. In a large bowl, beat the eggs with the milk, salt and pepper. Mix in the corn. Stir in the flour and baking powder.

2. Coat a large nonstick skillet with vegetable cooking spray. Heat over medium heat. Drop tablespoonsful of batter into the hot skillet and cook, turning once, until browned, about 5 minutes. Serve 2 per person.

Corn Pudding

Here's a classic made low-cal with skim milk and egg whites in place of whole eggs. Use fresh sweet corn in the summer and frozen kernels in winter, so you can enjoy it all year round.

6 SERVINGS   9% CALORIES FROM FAT   139 CALORIES PER SERVING

4 cups fresh corn kernels (from 4 to 6 ears of corn) or 2 packages (10
 ounces each) frozen corn, thawed
1 tablespoon flour
1 cup skim milk
¼ teaspoon salt
¼ teaspoon freshly ground pepper
3 egg whites

1. In a large saucepan, stir the corn kernels and flour until well blended. Pour in the milk and bring to a boil, stirring over medium-high heat. Reduce the heat to medium-low and simmer, partially covered, stirring occasionally, until the milk is thickened and the corn is tender, 3 to 5 minutes. Season with the salt and pepper. Transfer to a large bowl and let cool to room temperature.

2. Preheat the oven to 375° F. Beat the egg whites until stiff but not dry. Gently fold the egg whites into the corn mixture. Pour into an 8 × 11-inch baking dish.

3. Bake the corn pudding 20 to 25 minutes, until set and lightly browned on top.

Red Pepper Corn Fritters

One whole egg and one egg white rather than two whole eggs lightens this fritter batter without added cholesterol. Sweet red peppers contribute color and a sweet, mellow crunch.

4 SERVINGS   16% CALORIES FROM FAT   137 CALORIES PER SERVING

> 2 cups fresh corn kernels or 1 package (10 ounces) frozen corn, thawed
> 1 small red bell pepper, finely chopped
> 1 whole egg
> 1 egg white
> 2 tablespoons skim milk
> 1/2 teaspoon salt
> 1/8 teaspoon cayenne pepper
> 1/4 cup yellow cornmeal
> 1 tablespoon flour
> 1 teaspoon baking powder
> Vegetable cooking spray

1. In a large bowl, combine the corn kernels, red pepper, egg, egg white, milk, salt and cayenne. Mix well. Stir in the cornmeal, flour and baking powder just until blended.

2. Coat a large nonstick skillet with vegetable cooking spray. Heat over medium heat. Drop tablespoonsful of batter into the hot skillet and cook, turning once, until browned outside and cooked through, about 5 minutes.

Creamed Corn with Tomatoes

Use young, tender corn for this recipe. If the ears in your market look old or are imported from another state, increase the cooking time accordingly. Frozen or canned corn is a viable substitute, but nothing takes the place of the real thing. This is a late-summer treat, to be served with grilled or broiled fish, chicken or meat.

4 SERVINGS   9% CALORIES FROM FAT   133 CALORIES PER SERVING

4 ears of corn
2 tablespoons flour
1 cup skim milk
3 medium tomatoes, peeled, seeded and coarsely chopped
½ teaspoon salt
¼ teaspoon freshly ground pepper
¼ cup finely shredded fresh basil
Several drops of hot pepper sauce

1. Cut the corn kernels from the cob. Scrape the cobs with the back of a knife to press out all the "cream." Place all the corn in a medium nonstick saucepan.

2. Sprinkle the flour over the corn and stir to mix well. Set the pan over medium heat and cook, stirring constantly, until heated through, about 1 minute. Stir in the milk, raise the heat to medium-high and bring to a boil, stirring often.

3. Add the tomatoes to the saucepan and reduce the heat to medium-low. Season with the salt and pepper. Partially cover the pan and cook, stirring often, until the corn is tender and the sauce is thickened, about 10 minutes.

4. Stir in the basil and hot sauce and cook 1 minute longer. Serve at once.

Baked Stuffed Eggplant

4 Servings   27% Calories from fat   175 Calories per serving

2 medium eggplants (about 1 pound each), halved lengthwise
1½ tablespoons vegetable oil
1 medium onion, finely chopped
1 garlic clove, minced
3 medium tomatoes, peeled, seeded and chopped, or 1 can (16 ounces)
   whole peeled tomatoes, drained and chopped
2 tablespoons chopped parsley
¼ teaspoon salt
¼ teaspoon freshly ground pepper
2 tablespoons dry bread crumbs

1. Preheat the oven to 375° F. Using the tip of a knife, cut around the edge of the eggplant halves about ¼ inch from the skin, cutting about ½ inch deep. Place the eggplant halves, skin side-down, on a nonstick baking sheet and bake until tender but not collapsed, 30 to 45 minutes. Remove from the oven and let cool for about 10 minutes. (Leave the oven on.) As soon as the eggplant is cool enough to handle, scoop out the insides, leaving a ¼-inch shell intact. Coarsely chop the eggplant. Set the eggplant shells and chopped eggplant aside separately.

2. In a large nonreactive saucepan, heat the oil over medium-high heat. Add the onion and garlic and cook, stirring frequently, until softened and lightly colored, about 3 minutes. Add the tomatoes and cook, stirring often, until they give up their juice and then thicken slightly, about 5 minutes.

3. Stir in the chopped eggplant and parsley. Season the stuffing with the salt and pepper. Fill the eggplant shells with the stuffing, dividing evenly, and sprinkle ½ tablespoon bread crumbs over the top of each.

4. Return the eggplant to the oven and bake 15 to 17 minutes, until heated through and lightly browned on top.

Barbecued Green Beans

6 SERVINGS   28% CALORIES FROM FAT   61 CALORIES PER SERVING

$1^{1/2}$ *pounds green beans, trimmed and cut into* $1^{1/2}$-*inch pieces*
1 tablespoon butter
$^{1/2}$ *small onion, finely chopped*
$^{1/2}$ *small green bell pepper, finely chopped*
2 tablespoons bottled chili sauce or ketchup
2 tablespoons distilled white vinegar
1 teaspoon Dijon mustard
1 teaspoon curry powder
1 teaspoon prepared white horseradish
$^{1/8}$ *teaspoon cayenne pepper*

1. Bring a large pot of salted water to a boil. Add the beans and cook until just tender, about 5 minutes. Drain and rinse under cold running water. Set aside.

2. In a medium nonstick saucepan, melt the butter. Add the onions and pepper and cook over medium heat, stirring often, until softened, about 3 minutes. Stir in the chili sauce, vinegar, mustard, curry powder, horseradish and cayenne. Pour in 1 cup water, increase the heat to high and bring to a boil. Boil uncovered for 5 minutes.

3. Add the beans, reduce the heat to medium-low and simmer 5 minutes, or until the beans are very tender and the liquid in the pan is saucy. Serve at once.

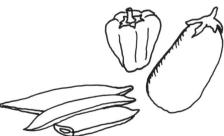

New Southern Green Beans

There's an old Southern country classic that stews big old green beans all day with salt pork and not a small amount of sugar. This modern, much lighter version, omits the fat and sugar and calls for tender beans, simmered briefly with just a bit of lean ham for flavor.

4 SERVINGS   32% CALORIES FROM FAT   57 CALORIES PER SERVING

> *1 pound green beans, trimmed and halved*
> *2 tablespoons fresh lemon juice*
> *2 teaspoons butter*
> *2 tablespoons finely chopped well-trimmed country or Black Forest ham*
> *¼ teaspoon salt*
> *¼ teaspoon freshly ground pepper*

1. Bring a large pot of salted water to a boil over high heat. Add the beans and cook, stirring occasionally, until tender, 5 to 7 minutes.

2. Meanwhile, place the lemon juice and butter in the bottom of a large serving bowl. Drain the beans and empty them into the bowl. Sprinkle the ham on top, season with the salt and pepper and toss well. Serve at once.

Stewed Mustard Greens

4 SERVINGS   9% CALORIES FROM FAT   59 CALORIES PER SERVING

> *2 pounds mustard greens*
> *3 medium tomatoes, peeled, seeded and chopped*
> *½ cup homemade chicken stock or reduced-sodium canned broth*
> *¼ teaspoon salt*
> *¼ teaspoon freshly ground pepper*

1. Wash the greens well in several changes of cold water to remove any grit. Tear off the tough stems on the bottom.

2. Bring a large pot of lightly salted water to a boil over high heat. Add the greens and return to a boil. Cook 3 minutes. Drain and rinse under cold running water. Squeeze out excess moisture and coarsely chop.

3. In a large nonreactive saucepan, combine the mustard greens with the tomatoes and chicken broth. Season with the salt and pepper. Partially cover and simmer over medium heat until tender, about 15 minutes. Serve at once.

— *Baked Grits with Onions and Tomato Sauce* —

Baked grits is a favorite Southern breakfast or brunch dish. Here we've cooked the grits in chicken stock and added onions and tomatoes for a light side dish that can be served as part of any meal.

6 SERVINGS   19% CALORIES FROM FAT   111 CALORIES PER SERVING

> 1½ *cups reduced-sodium canned chicken broth*
> ¾ *cup grits*
> ¼ *teaspoon salt*
> 2 *teaspoons canola oil*
> 1 *medium onion, finely chopped*
> 1 *garlic clove, minced*
> 3 *medium tomatoes, peeled, seeded and chopped, or 1 can (16 ounces)*
>   *whole peeled tomatoes, drained and chopped*
> *Vegetable cooking spray*

1. In a large saucepan, combine the broth with 1½ cups water. Bring to a boil over high heat. Stir in the grits and salt, reduce the heat to low and cook, stirring often, 15 minutes.

2. Meanwhile, heat the oil in a small saucepan over medium-high heat. Add the onion and garlic and cook, stirring often, until slightly softened, about 2 minutes. Stir in the tomatoes, reduce the heat to medium and cook, stirring often, until the tomato sauce is slightly thickened, about 5 minutes longer.

3. Preheat the oven to 350° F. Coat an 8 × 11-inch baking dish with vegetable cooking spray. Stir the tomato sauce into the grits and pour into the baking dish. Bake 30 minutes, or until slightly firm and bubbly.

— *Oven-Browned Grits with Parsley and Chives* —

With virtually no fat, these grits are a perfect accompaniment for grilled or roasted meats or chicken. Serve with quail at breakfast or brunch for a plantation-style Southern treat.

4 SERVINGS   6% CALORIES FROM FAT   77 CALORIES PER SERVING

> ½ cup grits
> ½ teaspoon salt
> ¼ teaspoon freshly ground pepper
> 1½ tablespoons chopped parsley
> 1½ tablespoons minced chives
> 2 teaspoons tomato paste
> Vegetable cooking spray

1. In a medium saucepan, bring 2½ cups water to a boil over high heat. Stir in the grits and season with the salt and pepper. Reduce the heat to low and cook, stirring often, 10 minutes. Stir in the herbs and tomato paste. Be sure the mixture is well blended. Cook, stirring occasionally, 5 minutes longer.

2. Coat a 9-inch-square nonstick baking pan with vegetable cooking spray. Turn the grits into the pan and spread evenly with a rubber spatula. Let stand until cooled to room temperature, about 15 minutes.

3. Preheat the broiler. Cut the grits into 6 rectangles, 3 × 4½ inches. With a wide spatula, transfer the grits to a nonstick baking sheet. Broil about 6 inches from the heat until lightly browned, 5 to 7 minutes.

Texas Cheese Grits

For an exotic touch, jalapeño peppers and Cheddar cheese add zip and flavor to the mild-tasting grits. There are some excellent brands of reduced-fat cheese that make this dish as welcome as the old-fashioned kind but with half the calories. Because these grits are baked without eggs, they should be spooned out for serving rather than cut into squares as is the case with more traditional baked grits.

6 TO 8 SERVINGS   28% CALORIES FROM FAT   152 CALORIES PER SERVING

> *Vegetable cooking spray*
> *1 cup skim milk*
> *¾ cup grits*
> *¼ teaspoon salt*
> *6 ounces reduced-fat Cheddar cheese, grated*
> *1 fresh jalapeño pepper, seeded and minced*

1. Preheat the oven to 350° F. Coat an 8 × 11-inch baking dish with vegetable cooking spray.

2. In a large saucepan, bring the milk and 2 cups water to a boil over high heat. Stir in the grits and salt. Reduce the heat to low and cook, stirring often, 15 minutes.

3. Stir the cheese and minced jalapeño into the grits and pour into the baking dish. Bake 30 minutes, or until slightly firm and lightly browned around the edges.

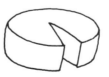

Pan-Fried Okra

In the Old South, this type of dish would always be deep-fried, most probably in lard. In the New South, we are as health conscious as anyone else, so I've created a much lightened version by crisping the okra in a very small amount of butter or oil in a nonstick skillet.

4 SERVINGS   27% CALORIES FROM FAT   162 CALORIES PER SERVING

¾ cup cornmeal
¼ teaspoon salt
¼ teaspoon freshly ground pepper
2 egg whites
¾ pound okra, cut into ½-inch pieces
4 teaspoons butter or vegetable oil

1. Preheat the oven to 250° F. In a medium bowl, mix the cornmeal with the salt and pepper. In another bowl, beat the egg whites lightly. Drop the okra into the egg whites and stir to coat the slices. Lift up with a large slotted spoon, letting the excess drip back into the bowl, and transfer to the cornmeal. Stir and toss to coat. Remove the coated slices, shaking off any excess.

2. In a large nonstick skillet, melt 2 teaspoons of the butter over medium heat. Add half of the okra and cook, turning and tossing frequently, until lightly browned and tender, about 7 minutes. Drain on paper towels, transfer to a nonstick baking sheet and keep warm in the oven.

3. Heat the remaining butter in the skillet and cook the remaining okra. Drain on paper towels. Combine both batches and serve at once while hot.

Elizabeth's Succotash

Butter beans are a small, flat species found at the height of summer throughout the South. Northerners like to make succotash with lima beans and usually without okra. Canned tomatoes are discouraged here. This is a dish that is meant to be served only when tomatoes are at their seasonal best.

4 SERVINGS   7% CALORIES FROM FAT   107 CALORIES PER SERVING

3 medium tomatoes, peeled, seeded and chopped
1 cup fresh or frozen corn kernels
1 cup cooked butter beans or baby lima beans
5 large okra, sliced ¼ inch thick
½ teaspoon salt
¼ teaspoon freshly ground pepper

1. In a medium nonstick saucepan, combine the tomatoes, corn, beans and okra. Cook over medium-low heat, stirring frequently, until the okra is tender and the tomatoes have given off all their liquid, about 10 minutes.

2. Season with the salt and pepper. Serve hot.

Baked Okra Parmesan

4 SERVINGS   44% CALORIES FROM FAT   85 CALORIES PER SERVING

1 pound okra, sliced in half lengthwise
1 tablespoon safflower or canola oil
2 tablespoons grated Parmesan cheese
¼ teaspoon freshly ground pepper

1. Preheat the oven to 350° F. Place the okra on a large baking sheet, cut sides up. Lightly brush the tops with the oil. Sprinkle the Parmesan cheese lightly over the okra. Season with the pepper.

2. Bake the okra 12 minutes, or until lightly browned and tender.

Pumpkin Buttermilk Spoonbread

Somewhat akin to a soufflé, spoonbread is so-called because it is sometimes made very soft and actually spooned out as a side dish like rice or creamed corn. In this easy recipe, we've added more egg whites than yolks to lighten the batter. The mixture puffs up slightly as it bakes, then deflates, leaving behind a moist and flavorful bread.

8 TO 10 SERVINGS   16% CALORIES FROM FAT   110 CALORIES PER SERVING

1¼ cups buttermilk
1¼ cups skim milk
½ cup fresh or canned unsweetened pumpkin puree
1 cup cornmeal
¼ teaspoon cinnamon
¼ teaspoon grated nutmeg
½ teaspoon salt
¼ teaspoon pepper
Vegetable cooking spray
2 whole eggs
3 egg whites

1. In a large saucepan, combine the buttermilk, skim milk and pumpkin puree. Cook over medium heat, stirring often, until just warmed through, about 5 minutes.

2. Add the cornmeal and cook, stirring often until thickened, about 5 minutes. Remove from the heat and stir in the cinnamon, nutmeg, salt and pepper. Pour into a large bowl and let cool for 10 to 15 minutes.

3. Meanwhile, preheat the oven to 400° F. Coat an 8 × 11-inch baking dish with vegetable cooking spray. Beat the whole eggs with the egg whites until mixed well and frothy. Stir into the cornmeal mixture and pour into the baking dish.

4. Bake 30 minutes, or until the spoonbread is set in the center and lightly browned. Cut into squares and serve at once.

Southern Cornbread Stuffing

This stuffing makes about 5 cups, enough to fill the cavity of a small turkey or large chicken for roasting. Be sure to season with lots of salt and pepper for an authentic Southern touch. Use to stuff a 12- to 14-pound turkey or serve with the Lemon-Rosemary Roasted Turkey Breast on page 69.

Baked Stuffed Vidalia Onions

Until just a few years ago, Vidalia was a word used to describe the football team my high school played against every year when I was growing up in Georgia. Now it means sweet onion! Thanks to smart marketing, Vidalia onions have become a much-sought-after delicacy throughout the country. Very sweet and mild, I find them hard to beat even baked plain. Here they are all dressed up with a seasoned bread crumb stuffing enlivened with just enough smoky bacon for flavor.

4 SERVINGS   30% CALORIES FROM FAT   174 CALORIES PER SERVING

> *4 Vidalia or other sweet onions (6 to 8 ounces each)*
> *2 thin slices of lean bacon, cut into 1/4-inch dice*
> *1/2 cup dry bread crumbs*
> *1 tablespoon finely chopped scallions*
> *1 teaspoon minced fresh savory or 1/2 teaspoon dried*
> *1 tablespoon fresh lemon juice*
> *1/4 teaspoon salt*
> *1/4 teaspoon freshly ground pepper*

1. Preheat the oven to 275° F. Trim the roots off the onions so that they stand upright but leave the skin intact. Set the onions upright in a 9-inch-square baking dish and add enough water to measure 1 inch deep. Bake 2 hours, or until the onions are very tender but still hold their shape. Remove from the oven and let cool slightly (The recipe can be prepared ahead to this point.)

2. Preheat the oven or increase the temperature to 350° F. Bring a small saucepan of water to a boil. Add the bacon and cook about 30 seconds. Drain and rinse briefly under running water. Pat dry on a paper towel.

3. As soon as you can handle the onions, pull back the brown skins and cut off at the bottom. Scoop out about 1 inch from the center of the onion; finely chop the scooped-out onion.

4. In a small bowl, combine the bread crumbs, scallions, savory, lemon juice, salt, pepper, bacon and chopped onion. Mix well. Fill the onions with the stuffing.

5. Set in a small nonstick baking dish and bake 5 to 7 minutes, or until heated through and lightly browned on top.

Black-Eyed Peas

Peas and beans grow well in the warm Southern climate. To preserve the bounty of summer's crop, frugal Southerners learned to dry these legumes as a means of preserving in the days before freezers and canning. Black-eyed peas are by far the most popular of these vegetables. To make a lighter version of the classic, we've cooked the peas in chicken stock and added some lean ham for flavor.

6 SERVINGS   9% CALORIES FROM FAT   156 CALORIES PER SERVING

> ½ *pound dried black-eyed peas*
> 3 *cups reduced-sodium canned chicken broth*
> ½ *cup lean boiled ham, cut into small dice*
> 1 *tablespoon chopped parsley*
> 1 *garlic clove, minced*
> ½ *teaspoon salt*
> ¼ *teaspoon freshly ground pepper*
> ⅛ *teaspoon hot pepper sauce, or to taste*

1. Rinse the black-eyed peas and pick over to remove any grit. Place in a large bowl and pour in enough cold water to cover. Soak overnight, changing the water every few hours. Drain and transfer to a medium saucepan.

2. Add the chicken broth to the peas and bring to a boil over high heat. Reduce the heat to medium-low, stir in the ham, parsley and garlic. Cook, stirring occasionally, until tender, about 45 minutes. Season with salt, pepper and hot sauce.

Hoppin' John

New Year's Day without a bowl of Hoppin' John is unheard of down South. To enjoy this simple dish of rice and black-eyed peas on that day means good luck throughout the year. In this lightened version, I've used more rice than beans and cooked the rice in chicken broth to give it a little extra character. I've added a little lean boiled ham for flavor. In my home, we don't limit this dish to holiday festivities. The combination of rice and beans is known to be an excellent source of meatless protein without fat.

6 TO 8 SERVINGS   6% CALORIES FROM FAT   170 CALORIES PER SERVING

¼ pound dried black-eyed peas (about ¾ cup)
1 garlic clove, minced
½ teaspoon dried thyme leaves
1 cup long-grain white rice
2 cups reduced-sodium canned chicken broth
1 tablespoon chopped parsley
2 ounces lean, well-trimmed country or Black Forest ham, finely chopped (about ½ cup)
½ teaspoon salt
¼ teaspoon freshly ground pepper

1. Rinse the black-eyed peas and pick them over to remove any grit. Place in a medium bowl and add enough cold water to cover. Soak overnight, changing the water every few hours. Drain well and transfer to a small saucepan. Cover with cold water by 2 inches and add the garlic and thyme. Bring to a simmer over medium-high heat. Reduce the heat to medium and cook, partially covered, stirring occasionally, until tender, 30 to 45 minutes.

2. Meanwhile, place the rice in a medium saucepan. Pour in the chicken broth and bring to a boil over high heat. Reduce the heat to medium-low and cook, covered, for 20 minutes. Stir with a fork, cover again and let stand for 5 minutes.

3. Drain the black-eyed peas and place them in a large serving bowl. Add the rice, parsley and ham. Season with the salt and pepper and stir to blend. Serve at once.

Cinnamon-Baked Squash

Sweet spice adds a piquant touch to yellow squash and costs nothing in added fat or calories. This recipe goes especially well with most pork dishes.

4 Servings   37% Calories from fat   38 Calories per serving

> *3 medium yellow squash*
> *1 tablespoon melted butter*
> *½ teaspoon cinnamon*
> *¼ teaspoon salt*
> *¼ teaspoon freshly ground pepper*

1. Preheat the oven to 350° F. Scrub the squash well and pat dry. Trim and cut crosswise on the diagonal into ¼-inch slices.

2. Arrange the slices of squash in a single layer on a large nonstick baking sheet. Brush lightly with the melted butter and sprinkle the cinnamon evenly over the squash. Season with the salt and pepper.

3. Bake 8 to 10 minutes, or until the squash is tender. Serve hot.

Creamy Squash Casserole

Rich, creamy foods are a traditional part of Southern cuisine, and even when you're eating light, there are times when nothing else will do. Luckily, skim milk and low-fat cottage cheese can produce much the same effect—without all the cholesterol and calories. Use only young, tender yellow squash here, or substitute small zucchini.

6 SERVINGS   37% CALORIES FROM FAT   133 CALORIES PER SERVING

Vegetable cooking spray
1 medium onion, thinly sliced
5 to 6 small yellow squash (1¾ pounds), cut into 1-inch chunks
2 tablespoons butter
2 tablespoons flour
1 cup skim milk
½ teaspoon salt
½ teaspoon freshly ground pepper
1 cup low-fat cottage cheese
1 egg
¼ cup bread crumbs

1. Preheat the oven to 350° F. Coat a large nonstick skillet with vegetable cooking spray. Add the onion and cook over medium-high heat, stirring occasionally, until slightly softened, about 2 minutes. Add the squash and cook, stirring and tossing, until almost tender, about 5 minutes. Remove from the heat and set aside.

2. In a small saucepan, melt the butter over medium heat. Add the flour and cook, stirring, about 1 minute. Whisk in the milk, raise the heat to medium-high and bring to a boil, whisking until thickened and smooth, 1 to 2 minutes. Reduce the heat to low and simmer, stirring often, 2 minutes longer. Remove from the heat and season with the salt and pepper. Set the white sauce aside.

3. In a food processor, puree the cottage cheese with the egg until smooth. In a large bowl, combine the sautéed squash and onion with the white sauce and the cottage cheese mixture. Stir well to blend. Turn the mixture into a 2-quart casserole or an 8 × 11-inch baking dish. Sprinkle the bread crumbs over the top.

4. Bake 25 minutes, or until the casserole is bubbly and the top is lightly browned.

— *Yellow Squash with Rice, Ham and Tomatoes* —

6 SERVINGS   24% CALORIES FROM FAT   107 CALORIES PER SERVING

3 medium yellow squash
1 tablespoon canola or safflower oil
1 small onion, finely chopped
1 medium tomato, peeled, seeded and chopped
½ cup rice
1 ounce trimmed country or Black Forest ham, cut into ¼-inch dice
   (about ¼ cup)
¼ teaspoon salt
¼ teaspoon freshly ground pepper
2 tablespoons chopped parsley

1. Halve the squash lengthwise and with a small spoon scrape out the seeds to form a small cavity. In a large pot of boiling salted water, cook the squash until barely tender, about 3 minutes. Transfer to paper towels to drain and set aside.

2. In a medium nonstick saucepan, heat the oil over medium heat. Add the onion and cook, stirring occasionally, until tender, about 3 minutes. Stir in the tomato, rice, ham and ½ cup water. Season with the salt and pepper, cover, reduce the heat to medium-low and cook until the rice is tender, about 20 minutes. Remove the cover, stir gently, cover again and let stand for 5 minutes off the heat.

3. Preheat the oven to 350° F. Arrange the squash cut sides-up in a large nonstick baking dish. Fill the cavities with about 2 tablespoonsful of the rice mixture.

4. Bake until heated through, about 10 minutes. Garnish with the parsley and serve at once.

Puree of Sweet Potatoes and Apples with Ginger

Apples complement the flavor of sweet potatoes and give a light, silky texture to this puree. Ginger is an old-fashioned Southern seasoning, which goes well with the two main ingredients. This is a subtle dish that needs little embellishment. Serve with turkey or chicken and collard greens, mustard greens or spinach.

6 TO 8 SERVINGS   3% CALORIES FROM FAT   155 CALORIES PER SERVING

4 medium sweet potatoes, peeled and cut into 1-inch dice
2 medium baking apples (preferably Golden Delicious), peeled, cored and cut into 1-inch pieces
½ teaspoon ground ginger
½ teaspoon salt
¼ teaspoon freshly ground pepper
1 tablespoon minced crystallized ginger (optional)

1. Place the sweet potatoes and apples in a large saucepan. Pour in enough cold water to cover. Add ¼ teaspoon salt and bring to a boil over medium-high heat. Reduce the heat to medium and cook until the sweet potatoes are tender, 15 to 20 minutes. Drain well.

2. Place the sweet potatoes and apples in a food processor and puree until smooth. Return to the saucepan and gently warm over low heat. Season with the ground ginger and the remaining ¼ teaspoon salt and the pepper. Stir in the crystallized ginger and serve hot.

Pan-Fried Green Tomatoes

We *do* eat a lot of green tomatoes in the South—I guess because there are so many of them almost all year round. Of course, early summer or fall is the best time to look for them in most gardens. Traditionally, the slices are heavily coated and fried in bacon fat. To lighten the recipe, I've used egg whites, rather than whole eggs, and browned the tomatoes in just a small amount of oil. The result is a crunchy outside with a moist, tender center. Try them with pork chops and corn pudding.

4 SERVINGS   25% CALORIES FROM FAT   159 CALORIES PER SERVING

> *¾ cup cornmeal*
> *¼ teaspoon salt*
> *¼ teaspoon freshly ground pepper*
> *2 egg whites*
> *3 medium green tomatoes, cut into ¼-inch slices*
> *4 teaspoons butter*

1. In a shallow bowl, mix the cornmeal with the salt and pepper. In another bowl, lightly beat the egg whites until frothy. Dip the green tomato slices in the egg whites, letting the excess drip back into the bowl. Then dredge in the seasoned cornmeal to coat both sides; gently shake off any excess.

2. In a large nonstick skillet, melt 2 teaspoons of the butter over medium heat. Add half the tomato slices in a single layer and cook, turning occasionally, until lightly browned and tender, about 6 minutes. Drain on paper towels. Repeat with the remaining butter and tomatoes.

Baked Tomatoes, Zucchini and Onions

4 SERVINGS   48% CALORIES FROM FAT   97 CALORIES PER SERVING

3 medium tomatoes
2 large zucchini (1 pound)
2 medium onions
1½ tablespoons vegetable oil
¼ teaspoon salt
¼ teaspoon freshly ground pepper
1 teaspoon dried thyme leaves

1. Preheat the oven to 350° F. Use a serrated knife to cut the tomatoes into ⅛-inch-thick slices. Slice the zucchini on the diagonal to measure the same thickness. Cut the onions into thin slices so that all three vegetables are of uniform thickness.

2. On a nonstick baking sheet, alternate the slices of tomato, zucchini and onion in 2 long, overlapping rows. Drizzle the oil over the vegetables and season with the salt, pepper and thyme.

3. Bake until lightly browned and tender, 12 to 15 minutes. Use a long spatula to lift and remove individual portions of the layered vegetables to serving plates.

QUICK BREADS AND BISCUITS

In the heat of the South in the days before air conditioning, anything quick in the kitchen was greatly appreciated. Out of this tradition come wonderful recipes for cornbread, biscuits and quick breads, enhanced with fruits, nuts and fresh vegetables. Batter was made with a few quick strokes of a spoon, with baking powder instead of yeast, saving all-important, scarce energy on a sultry day.

Reducing the fat and calories in baking is not easy. I've lightened my cornbread by using skim milk, reducing the amount of eggs in the batter and using minimum amounts of butter or bacon fat for flavor. And just for the record, we Southerners have never added sugar; that's a Yankee tradition. This is a savory cornbread to be enjoyed with meals.

With biscuits, the amount of baking powder and soda has been increased slightly to compensate for the reduction in the shortening traditionally used. The result is a quick-rising, delightful biscuit that is as crispy and light as those that use twice as much fat. And with calories in mind, use a smaller 2-inch, rather than 3-inch, cutter for making biscuits. Two or three smaller ones with a meal can be as satisfying as larger versions. Likewise, muffins are made in 1½-inch mini-muffin, or gem, pans.

Banana Bread, Date Nut Bread and Sweet Potato Bread can be served like cornbread or biscuits as a savory with meals, or for breakfast or as a dessert. They are all loaf breads that will serve 10 to 12, and they are excellent for gift giving.

Banana Bread

Use the ripest, brownest bananas possible for full flavor. Served with low-fat yogurt, this makes a satisfying light dessert. Homemade banana bread makes a nice gift, too.

10 TO 12 SERVINGS   5% CALORIES FROM FAT   160 CALORIES PER SERVING

Vegetable cooking spray
2 cups flour
½ cup brown sugar
1 teaspoon baking powder
1 teaspoon baking soda
¼ teaspoon salt
½ cup skim milk
1 egg
2 very ripe bananas (about 1½ cups), smashed
½ teaspoon fresh lemon juice

1. Preheat the oven to 350° F. Coat a 9 × 5 × 3-inch loaf pan, preferably nonstick, with vegetable cooking spray. Combine the flour, brown sugar, baking powder, baking soda and salt in a mixing bowl. Stir well to blend. Pour in the milk and egg and with a mixer on low speed, beat, scraping down the sides as needed, until blended. Add the bananas and lemon juice and mix again until smooth. Be careful not to overbeat or the bread will be tough.

2. Pour the batter into the prepared loaf pan and bake for 1 hour and 10 minutes, or until a toothpick inserted in the center comes out clean.

Cornbread

Cornbread is the most Southern of all quick breads. Traditionally made with a generous douse of bacon drippings and whole milk, our version is just as flavorful with half the amount of fat. Cornbread is often served with "pot liquor," the broth left from long-cooking greens. For a similar effect, try serving cornbread with your favorite soup as a meal in itself. Otherwise, serve as part of any traditional Southern menu for authentic appeal.

9 SERVINGS   22% CALORIES FROM FAT   149 CALORIES PER SERVING

> *Vegetable cooking spray*
> *1 cup cornmeal, preferably yellow*
> *1 cup all-purpose flour*
> *1 tablespoon baking powder*
> *½ teaspoon salt*
> *2 tablespoons melted bacon fat or butter*
> *1 cup skim milk*
> *1 egg, beaten*

1. Preheat the oven to 425° F. Coat a 9-inch-square nonstick baking pan with vegetable cooking spray. In a medium bowl, combine the cornmeal, flour, baking powder and salt. Stir well to blend. In a separate bowl, beat the melted butter, milk and egg until well mixed. Pour into the dry ingredients and with several quick strokes of a wooden spoon, stir to form a thick batter.

2. Pour the batter into the prepared pan and bake for 20 minutes, or until a toothpick inserted in the center comes out clean. Let cool for 10 minutes before cutting into 9 large squares.

Cornbread with Cheddar Cheese and Jalapeño Pepper

12 SERVINGS   29% CALORIES FROM FAT   142 CALORIES PER SERVING

Vegetable cooking spray
1 cup yellow or white cornmeal
1 cup all-purpose flour
1 tablespoon baking powder
½ teaspoon salt
2 tablespoons melted butter
1 cup skim milk
1 egg, beaten
1 cup grated reduced-fat cheddar cheese
1 fresh jalapeño pepper, seeded and minced

1. Preheat the oven to 425° F. Coat a 9-inch-square nonstick baking pan with vegetable cooking spray. In a medium bowl, combine the cornmeal, flour, baking powder and salt. Stir well to blend. In a separate bowl, beat the melted butter, milk and egg until well mixed. Stir in the cheese and ja-lapeño pepper. Add to the dry ingredients and with several quick strokes of a wooden spoon, stir to form a thick batter.

2. Pour the batter into the prepared pan and bake for 20 minutes, or until a toothpick inserted in the center comes out clean. Let the cornbread stand for 10 minutes before cutting into 12 small squares.

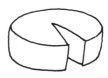

Cornbread with Fresh Corn and Tomato

9 SERVINGS   21% CALORIES FROM FAT   166 CALORIES PER SERVING

Vegetable cooking spray
1 cup yellow or white cornmeal
1 cup all-purpose flour
3 teaspoons baking powder
½ teaspoon salt
2 tablespoons melted butter
1 cup skim milk
1 egg, beaten
1 cup fresh or thawed frozen corn kernels
1 ripe medium tomato, peeled, seeded and chopped

1. Preheat the oven to 425° F. Coat a 9-inch-square nonstick baking pan with vegetable cooking spray.

2. In a medium bowl, combine the cornmeal, flour, baking powder and salt. Stir well to blend. In a separate bowl, beat the melted butter, milk and egg until blended. Stir in the corn and tomato. Pour into the dry ingredients and with several quick strokes of a wooden spoon, stir to form a thick batter.

3. Pour the batter into the prepared pan and bake for 20 minutes, or until a toothpick inserted in the center comes out clean. Let cool for 10 minutes before cutting into 9 large or 18 small squares.

Date Nut Bread

14 Servings   13% Calories from fat   157 Calories per serving

Vegetable cooking spray
1 cup chopped dates
½ cup sugar
2 tablespoons butter
1 cup boiling water
2¼ cups flour
1 teaspoon baking powder
1 teaspoon baking soda
½ teaspoon salt
1 egg
1 teaspoon vanilla extract
¼ cup chopped pecans

1. Preheat the oven to 325° F. Coat an 8 × 4 × 2½-inch loaf pan with vegetable cooking spray. In a large bowl, combine the dates, sugar and butter. Pour the boiling water over the dates. Stir to dissolve the sugar and melt the butter. Let stand until cooled to room temperature.

2. Add the flour, baking powder, baking soda, salt, nuts, egg and vanilla to the date mixture and stir well to blend. Stir in the nuts. Pour into the prepared pan and bake for about 50 minutes, or until a toothpick inserted in the center of the bread comes out clean.

Sweet Potato Bread

Sweet potatoes give this quick bread a light and colorful texture with a uniquely rich flavor. Thinly sliced and served with coffee, this loaf makes a delightful morning treat.

12 SERVINGS   18% CALORIES FROM FAT   151 CALORIES PER SERVING

> *2 medium sweet potatoes (about 1 pound)*
> *1½ cups flour*
> *½ cup brown sugar*
> *1 teaspoon baking powder*
> *1 teaspoon baking soda*
> *¼ teaspoon salt*
> *¼ teaspoon grated nutmeg*
> *¼ teaspoon cinnamon*
> *½ cup skim milk*
> *1 egg*
> *2 tablespoons vegetable oil*
> *Vegetable cooking spray*

1. Peel the sweet potatoes and cut them into 1-inch cubes. Place in a medium saucepan and add enough water to cover. Boil over medium-high heat until tender, about 10 minutes. Drain and puree the sweet potatoes in a food processor.

2. Preheat the oven to 350° F. In a medium bowl, combine the flour, brown sugar, baking powder, baking soda, salt, nutmeg and cinnamon. In a separate bowl, blend together the pureed sweet potatoes, milk, egg and oil. Add to the dry ingredients and stir with a wooden spoon until the mixture forms a smooth batter. Do not overwork the batter or the bread will be tough.

3. Coat an 8 × 4 × 2½-inch loaf pan with vegetable cooking spray. Pour in the batter and smooth the top with the back of a spoon. Bake 1 hour, or until a toothpick inserted in the center comes out clean.

Buttermilk Cornmeal Muffins

This same batter can be used to make corn sticks. Corn stick molds are cast-iron implements that simulate the form of small ears of corn. Coat with vegetable cooking spray and heat the molds in the hot oven for a few minutes before spooning in the batter.

MAKES 24 MINI-MUFFINS   24% CALORIES FROM FAT   43 CALORIES PER MUFFIN

Vegetable cooking spray
1 egg
1 cup buttermilk
1 tablespoon canola oil
¾ cup all-purpose flour
¾ cup white or yellow cornmeal
½ teaspoon salt
2 teaspoons baking soda
1 teaspoon baking powder

1. Preheat the oven to 425° F. Coat 2 mini-muffin tins (24 molds) with vegetable cooking spray.

2. In a medium bowl, beat the egg with the buttermilk and oil until well blended. In a large bowl, stir together the flour, cornmeal, salt, baking soda and baking powder until blended. Add the buttermilk mixture and stir with a wooden spoon just until the mixture is smooth.

3. Spoon the batter into the muffin tins and bake 15 minutes, or until a toothpick inserted in the center comes out clean. Turn out onto a wire rack while hot.

Buttermilk Biscuits

Buttermilk is low in fat and gives a decidedly tart, cheesy flavor to regular biscuits. These are best served right from the oven. Day-old biscuits can be split in half and toasted.

MAKES 16 BISCUITS   18% CALORIES FROM FAT   90 CALORIES PER BISCUIT

> *2½ cups all-purpose flour*
> *1 tablespoon baking powder*
> *1 teaspoon baking soda*
> *½ teaspoon salt*
> *2 tablespoons butter*
> *1 cup buttermilk*

1. Preheat the oven to 425° F. In a food processor, combine the flour, baking powder, baking soda and salt. Pulse briefly to mix. Add the butter and process in several quick pulses until the mixture resembles the texture of coarse meal. With the machine on, add the buttermilk all at once. Process just until the dough forms a ball around the blades.

2. Turn out the dough onto a lightly floured work surface and knead for about 10 seconds. Roll out ½ inch thick. Use a 2-inch round cookie cutter to form 16 biscuits.

3. Arrange the biscuits on a nonstick baking sheet and bake for 10 to 12 minutes, or until lightly browned on top.

Country Biscuits

<small>MAKES ABOUT 16 BISCUITS   17% CALORIES FROM FAT   90 CALORIES PER BISCUIT</small>

2½ cups all-purpose flour
2 teaspoons baking powder
1 teaspoon baking soda
½ teaspoon salt
2 tablespoons vegetable shortening
1 cup skim milk

1. Preheat the oven to 425° F. In a food processor, combine the flour, baking powder, baking soda and salt. Pulse briefly to mix. Add the shortening and process in several quick pulses until the mixture resembles the texture of coarse meal. With the machine on, add the milk all at once. Process just until the dough forms a ball around the blades.

2. Turn out the dough onto a lightly floured work surface and knead for about 10 seconds. Roll out ½ inch thick. Use a 2-inch cookie cutter to form small biscuits.

3. Arrange the biscuits on a nonstick baking sheet and bake 10 to 12 minutes, or until browned.

Chapter Eight

DESSERTS

Southerners have a sweet tooth. Pies, cakes, candies and confections are as much a part of the Southern table as barbecue and grits. In Georgia, summer was a special time when peaches were always ripe and watermelon was always cold and crisp. And dessert was always important.

It was a challenge to recreate some of my favorite sweets using a minimum of sugar and fat. Of course, lots of fruits help. They are nutritious, light and delicious, especially in season. Melons, peaches, plums, figs, blackberries and blueberries are summertime favorites. And nothing can beat fall apples and pears. Florida provides its neighbors with a bounty of winter citrus fruits. The recipe for Florida Grapefruit and Oranges with Honey is an example of how refreshing and lean this kind of dessert can be.

Less butter, fewer eggs, skim milk and less sugar have been used to make traditional favorites lighter. Blackberry Crumble uses only a minimum amount of butter to form a crisp topping. Key Lime Cheese Cakes have a graham cracker crust made with just enough butter to hold it together. Peach Sherbet is made with skim milk, with delicious results. And Meringue Plum Cake with Sherry does away with egg yolks altogether to make a light, angel food cake–like dessert flavored with sherry.

Bourbon is as likely to be found in a Southerner's kitchen as is vanilla extract. Rum has long been popular around these parts, especially in coastal areas. Old recipes for ambrosia, egg-nog, rich charlottes and cake fillings call for sherry as a flavoring. Using spirits is a good way to give character and taste to desserts without expending a lot of calories.

Peaches Poached in Bourbon is a great example of how to achieve this kind of balance.

Our frugal Southern ancestors in the late eighteenth and early nineteenth centuries learned that good food comes from using the best of what the land has to offer. That tradition lives on today. We don't have to give up desserts to enjoy lighter fare. We just have to be appreciative of the best of what is in season, and a bit more creative and resourceful in the use of traditional flavorings.

— *Baked Apples with Bourbon and Pecans* —

Baked fruit is packed with flavor and remarkably light. Bourbon gives a mellow touch here that marries well with a few chopped nuts. If time permits, roast the pecans for a few minutes in a moderate (350° F) oven until lightly browned. Sprinkle a few extra drops of bourbon over the apples just before serving, if you like. This replaces some of the flavor that burns off during cooking.

4 SERVINGS   27% CALORIES FROM FAT   155 CALORIES PER SERVING

4 medium baking apples
2 tablespoons sugar
1 teaspoon fresh lemon juice
¼ cup pecans, finely chopped
1 egg white
½ cup bourbon
½ cup boiling water

1. Preheat the oven to 375° F. Core the apples to within ½ inch of their bottoms and place in an 8-inch-square baking dish.

2. In a small bowl, stir together the sugar, lemon juice, pecans and egg white. Fill each apple with about 1 tablespoon of the nut mixture. Pour the bourbon and boiling water into the bottom of the baking dish.

3. Bake the apples uncovered, basting often with the pan juices, 30 to 45 minutes, or until the apples are soft but not mushy. Serve warm, at room temperature or cold.

Ambrosia

Ambrosia is a festive dish served at Thanksgiving and Christmas, when oranges and grapefruit are in season. We've cut back on the amount of coconut traditionally used and added kumquats for extra color and flavor. If these tart, oval-shaped citrus fruits are not available, use tangerines or clementines instead. Serve well chilled, in glass or crystal bowls.

6 Servings   14% Calories from fat   161 Calories per serving

> 3 large oranges
> 1 large pink grapefruit
> 4 kumquats, quartered lengthwise
> ½ cup flaked coconut
> ¼ cup sugar
> ½ cup dry sherry

1. Cut off the tops and bottoms of the oranges. With a small, sharp stainless steel knife, cut off the skin and white pith in a circular motion, moving from top to bottom. Cut out the sections from between the membranes, remove all seeds and place the orange sections in a large bowl.

2. Peel and section the grapefruit as you did the oranges. Work over the bowl of orange sections to catch all the juices. Add the grapefruit sections to the oranges.

3. Add the kumquats, coconut, sugar and sherry to the citrus. Stir gently to blend. Cover and refrigerate for at least 1 hour, until chilled. Serve in chilled bowls.

Figs with Lemon Cream

Figs grow well in the sultry South. This is a simple recipe that is flavorful and visually very attractive. Garnish with fresh mint leaves or a curl of lemon rind for a touch of color.

4 Servings   30% Calories from fat   107 Calories per serving

4 ripe fresh figs
3 ounces light cream cheese or Neufchâtel cheese, softened
2 tablespoons sugar
1 tablespoon fresh lemon juice

1. Cut the figs lengthwise into quarters, leaving them attached at the bottom. Wrap in plastic wrap and refrigerate 2 to 3 hours, until well chilled.

2. In a small bowl, beat the cream cheese together with the sugar and lemon juice. Gently pry open the figs to expose the red interior. Set each fig on a dessert plate. Spoon 1 heaping tablespoonful of the lemon cream into the center of each and serve at once.

Banana Pudding with Rum

8 TO 10 SERVINGS   12% CALORIES FROM FAT   169 CALORIES PER SERVING

½ cup plus 2 tablespoons sugar
¼ cup all-purpose flour
⅛ teaspoon salt
2 eggs, separated
1½ cups skim milk
¼ cup rum
3 ripe bananas, sliced
15 vanilla wafers

1. Preheat the oven to 425° F. In a double boiler, combine ½ cup of the sugar with the flour and salt. Mix in the egg yolks, milk and rum. Cook over high heat, stirring constantly, until thickened, about 3 minutes. Reduce the heat to medium and cook, stirring often, 3 minutes longer.

2. Spread half the custard in the bottom of an 8 × 11-inch baking dish. Cover with a layer of banana slices and top with the vanilla wafers. Repeat with the remaining pudding mixture and bananas.

3. Beat the egg whites with the remaining 2 tablespoons sugar until stiff. Spoon this meringue over the pudding and bake until lightly browned, about 8 minutes. Let cool, then refrigerate for at least 2 hours, until chilled, before serving.

Blackberry Crumble

Blackberries are the ultimate Southern summer fruit. This recipe calls for just enough topping to give a little crunch and sweetness to the tart fruit. Let the crumble cool to room temperature before serving.

8 SERVINGS   22% CALORIES FROM FAT   185 CALORIES PER SERVING

4 cups fresh blackberries
2 tablespoons sugar
2 teaspoons fresh lemon juice
¾ cup plus 1 tablespoon all-purpose flour
½ cup firmly packed brown sugar
3 tablespoons butter

1. Preheat oven to 375° F. In a medium bowl, combine the berries with the sugar, lemon juice and 1 tablespoon flour. Stir to blend and spread out in a baking dish that measures 8 × 11 inches.

2. In a food processor, combine the remaining ¾ cup flour and brown sugar. Add the butter and pulse until the mixture resembles coarse cornmeal. Sprinkle this topping evenly over the berries.

3. Bake 30 minutes, or until lightly browned and bubbly.

Blueberry Cobbler

In the South, we love our biscuits so much, we even put them on top of our fruit and bake them into cobblers. A minimum of butter and sugar and low-fat buttermilk makes this homey dessert as light as it can be. If you can afford the extra 25 calories, top with a heaping tablespoon of nonfat vanilla frozen yogurt.

6 SERVINGS   18% CALORIES FROM FAT   195 CALORIES PER SERVING

1½ cups all-purpose flour
1 tablespoon baking powder
¼ cup plus 1 tablespoon sugar
¼ teaspoon salt
2 tablespoons cold butter, diced
¾ cup buttermilk
2 cups blueberries
2 teaspoons fresh lemon juice

1. In a food processor, combine the flour, baking powder, 1 tablespoon of the sugar and the salt. Pulse briefly to blend. Add the butter and process until the mixture resembles the texture of coarse cornmeal. With the machine on, pour in the buttermilk and process until the dough forms into a ball around the blades.

2. Turn out the dough onto a floured work surface and roll out into a circle that measures about ¼ inch thick. Use a 3-inch round cutter or the bottom of a drinking glass to make 6 biscuits. (Discard the scraps of dough or reserve for another use.) Place the biscuits on a plate and refrigerate for up to 3 hours until you are ready to assemble the dish.

3. Preheat the oven to 375° F. In a medium nonreactive saucepan, combine the blueberries with the remaining ¼ cup sugar and the lemon juice. Bring to a boil over medium-high heat, stirring often.

4. Pour the hot blueberries into an 8 × 11-inch baking dish. Arrange the biscuits evenly over the top. Bake for 30 minutes, or until the biscuits are lightly browned on top. Serve warm.

Mac's Bourbon Balls

Mac lived across the street from where I grew up in Georgia. She was an earthy character who you'd never expect to make the best bourbon balls in town. At Christmas, she would bring them over in a nice tin and we'd eat them all in about an hour. I've lightened up her recipe, which my mother kept all these years in an old shoebox. There is no substitute for vanilla wafers, so I've adapted the rest of the ingredients to work with only a few of these cookies and added proportionally more bourbon than Mac ever did!

6 SERVINGS   40% CALORIES FROM FAT   242 CALORIES PER SERVING

6 ounces vanilla wafers
½ cup powdered sugar
2 tablespoons chopped pecans
2 tablespoons butter, softened
¼ cup bourbon

1. In a food processor, grind the vanilla wafers to fine crumbs, about 30 seconds. Add ¼ cup of the powdered sugar, the pecans, butter and bourbon. Pulse until the mixture forms a ball around the blade, about 30 seconds longer.

2. Turn out the dough onto a work surface and pinch off small pieces, about 1 heaping teaspoonful each. Roll between your palms to form into round balls. Set on a nonstick baking sheet, cover with plastic wrap and refrigerate at least 1 hour, or overnight.

3. Before serving, roll the bourbon balls in the remaining ¼ cup sugar, shake off any excess and arrange on a platter.

Cantaloupe with Strawberries Macerated in Rum

4 SERVINGS   27% CALORIES FROM FAT   160 CALORIES PER SERVING

2 pints (4 cups) strawberries
2 tablespoons sugar
1 large cantaloupe, thoroughly chilled
¼ cup rum
Several sprigs of fresh mint, for garnish

1. Hull the berries and cut them into thin slices. Place in a medium bowl and sprinkle on the sugar.

2. Cut the melon in half and remove the seeds. Using a melon baller, scoop out as many small balls of cantaloupe as you can. Add the melon to the strawberries.

3. Pour the rum over the fruit and toss to mix well. Cover and refrigerate, stirring occasionally, at least 30 minutes and up to 2 hours. Serve chilled in dessert dishes, garnished with sprigs of mint.

Gingerbread

This is a light, airy version of the old-fashioned classic. Low-fat buttermilk gives a rich, tangy flavor. As it cooks, the gingerbread rises to a height of about 3 inches so that each portion is more substantial that it seems. Serve with low-fat yogurt for a healthy dessert.

12 SERVINGS   23% CALORIES FROM FAT   197 CALORIES PER SERVING

> *Vegetable cooking spray*
> *2½ cups all-purpose flour*
> *2 teaspoons baking soda*
> *2 teaspoons baking powder*
> *1 tablespoon ground ginger*
> *¼ teaspoon salt*
> *4 tablespoons butter, softened*
> *½ cup sugar*
> *2 eggs*
> *½ cup buttermilk*
> *¼ cup molasses*

1. Preheat the oven to 325° F. Coat the bottom of an 8-inch-square cake pan with vegetable cooking spray. In a large bowl, combine the flour, baking soda, baking powder, ginger and salt. In a large bowl, beat the butter with the sugar until creamy smooth. Add the eggs, beating well after each addition. Add the dry ingredients, alternating with the buttermilk and molasses, in two or three additions. Beat until smooth. Be careful not to overbeat or the gingerbread will be tough.

2. Pour the batter into the cake pan and bake for 45 minutes, or until a toothpick inserted in the center comes out clean. Cool in the pan for 10 minutes, then turn the gingerbread out to cool completely on a wire rack. Cut into 2-inch squares to serve.

— *Florida Grapefruit and Oranges with Honey* —

This is a surprisingly elegant dessert. Grating the zest, the colored part of the rind, is time consuming and somewhat tedious, but the results are worth the effort. The trick is to have all the ingredients as cold as possible and to use only the best of the winter fruit around. One pink and one white grapefruit will make this healthful citrus salad especially attractive.

4 SERVINGS   2% CALORIES FROM FAT   138 CALORIES PER SERVING

> *2 grapefruit*
> *2 or 3 navel oranges*
> *¼ cup honey*

1. With the small holes of a 4-sided hand grater, remove the zest from both grapefruit and from 2 of the oranges, trying to avoid as much of the bitter white pith as possible. Place the zest in a small saucepan of cold water. Bring to a boil over high heat and cook 2 minutes. Strain the zest through a fine-mesh sieve lined with a double layer of dampened cheesecloth. Rinse under cold running water, drain and scrape the zest from the cheesecloth into a small bowl; set aside.

2. Cut the tops and bottoms off the grapefruit and oranges. With a small, sharp, stainless steel knife, cut off the remaining skin and all the white pith. Working over a bowl to catch all the juices, cut down on either side of the membranes to remove the citrus sections. Remove any seeds and set the fruit aside. Squeeze the membranes and skins in a strainer set over the bowl and press down to extract all the juice. You need ½ cup. If there is less, squeeze the third orange to obtain the correct amount.

3. Add the honey to the citrus juices and whisk to blend well. Stir in the reserved grapefruit and orange zest. Add the citrus sections and stir gently to mix. Cover and refrigerate for at least 1 hour, or overnight, until well chilled.

4. To serve, arrange alternating sections of grapefruit and orange in a circular design on 4 chilled dessert plates. Spoon the sweetened juices in the bowl over the fruit and serve at once.

Key Lime Cheese Cakes

Key limes—small and yellowish, with a distinctive citrus flavor—are famous for the pie named after them. The fresh ones are hard to come by, though many specialty food shops carry the bottled juice. Regular green limes will work just fine in this recipe, though.

Even people eating lighter can enjoy these scrumptious individual cheese cakes, because the recipe adds a minimum of sugar and keeps calories and cholesterol down with low-fat evaporated milk and light cream cheese.

6 SERVINGS   38% CALORIES FROM FAT   139 CALORIES PER SERVING

8 graham cracker squares (about 2 ounces)
¼ cup plus 1 tablespoon sugar
1 tablespoon melted butter
½ teaspoon vanilla extract
Vegetable cooking spray
1 cup evaporated skim milk
4 ounces light cream cheese or Neufchâtel cheese, softened
½ cup fresh lime juice, preferably key lime
1 teaspoon grated lime zest

1. Preheat the oven to 350° F. Place the graham crackers in a food processor and grind to crumbs. Transfer to a medium bowl and stir in 1 tablespoon of the sugar, the melted butter and the vanilla. Stir with a fork until evenly blended and moistened.

2. Spray 6 attractive ½-cup ramekins with vegetable cooking spray. Divide the buttered crumbs evenly among the ramekins. Press gently to form a bottom crust in each. Bake 10 minutes, until the crust is crisp. Remove and let cool to room temperature.

3. In a medium saucepan, combine the evaporated milk, cream cheese, lime juice and remaining ¼ cup sugar. Cook over medium heat, stirring often, until slightly thickened, about 10 minutes.

4. Pour the cream cheese mixture into the ramekins, dividing evenly. Cover and refrigerate until set, at least 2 hours or overnight. Garnish the tops with a pinch of grated lime zest just before serving.

Peach Cobbler

6 Servings   13% Calories from fat   188 Calories per serving

½ cup plus 1 tablespoon all-purpose flour
¼ cup plus 2 tablespoons sugar
1 teaspoon baking powder
¼ teaspoon salt
1 tablespoon vegetable shortening
3 tablespoons skim milk
4 medium peaches, peeled and sliced, or 1 can (16 ounces) peach halves
    packed in light syrup, sliced
1 tablespoon fresh lemon juice
1 tablespoon instant tapioca

1. Preheat the oven to 375° F. In a food processor, combine the flour, 1 tablespoon of the sugar, the baking powder and the salt. Pulse briefly to blend. Add the shortening and process in several quick pulses until cut to the size of small peas. Add the milk and process until the dough forms a ball around the blades. Turn out the dough onto a lightly floured work surface. Roll out to ⅛ inch thick. Use a 2½- to 3-inch biscuit or cookie cutter to cut out 6 rounds.

2. In a medium bowl, combine the peaches, ¼ cup of the sugar, the lemon juice and the tapioca. Stir well and empty into an 8 × 11-inch baking dish. Arrange the biscuits on top and sprinkle the remaining 1 tablespoon sugar over the dough.

3. Bake until the biscuits are light brown and the peaches are bubbly, about 20 minutes. Serve at room temperature.

Peaches with Blackberry Sauce

4 SERVINGS   2% CALORIES FROM FAT   114 CALORIES PER SERVING

1 cup blackberries
2 tablespoons sugar
2 teaspoons fresh lemon juice
4 large, ripe peaches, peeled and sliced
4 small mint leaves, for garnish

1. Combine the blackberries, sugar and 1 teaspoon lemon juice in a food processor. Puree until smooth. To remove the seeds, pass the puree through a fine-mesh sieve into a bowl. Cover and refrigerate the blackberry sauce for at least 2 hours.

2. To serve, spoon about 1½ tablespoons of the sauce over the bottom of 4 dessert dishes. Toss the peach slices with the remaining lemon juice and arrange attractively on top. Garnish with the mint.

Caramelized Peaches

With perfect ripe fruit, sometimes the simplest dessert is the best. For an added treat, serve these scrumptious peaches over a scoop of nonfat vanilla frozen yogurt or chopped toasted almonds on top.

4 SERVINGS   29% CALORIES FROM FAT   172 CALORIES PER SERVING

4 large ripe peaches
2 tablespoons butter
¼ cup firmly packed brown sugar

1. Bring a large saucepan of water to a boil. Add the peaches and cook 15 to 45 seconds, until the skins begin to wrinkle. Remove with a skimmer or slotted spoon and drain in a colander. Rinse under cold running water until cool. Peel the peaches; the skins should slip off easily. Cut in half and remove the pits.

2. In a large nonstick skillet, melt the butter and brown sugar over medium heat, stirring until a syrup forms, 1 to 2 minutes. Add the peaches, cut sides-up, and cook, spooning the syrup and juices up over the fruit and carefully turning once or twice, until the peaches are glazed and tender, 6 to 8 minutes. Serve warm.

Peach Sherbet

6 SERVINGS   1% CALORIES FROM FAT   140 CALORIES PER SERVING

> *2 cups skim milk*
> *½ cup sugar*
> *4 large ripe peaches, peeled and quartered, or 1 can (16 ounces) peach*
>   *halves packed in light syrup, drained*

1. In a small saucepan, combine the milk and the sugar. Cook over medium-low heat, stirring often, until bubbles form around the edges and the sugar is dissolved, 4 to 5 minutes. Remove from the heat and let cool to room temperature.

2. In a food processor or blender, puree the peaches with the sweetened milk. Transfer to an ice cream maker and freeze according to the manufacturer's instructions. (Alternatively, place in an 8 × 11-inch baking dish and freeze, stirring occasionally, until slushy but not solid, about 5 hours. Return to the food processor and blend until smooth.) Place the sherbet in a covered container and freeze until solid, about 1 hour longer.

Peach Upside-Down Cake

8 Servings   15% Calories from fat   228 Calories per serving

1 cup all-purpose flour
½ cup sugar
1 teaspoon baking powder
¼ teaspoon salt
2 tablespoons butter, softened
½ cup skim milk
1 egg
1 teaspoon vanilla extract
4 peaches, peeled and quartered, or 1 can (16 ounces) peach halves
    packed in light syrup, drained and quartered
Vegetable cooking spray
½ cup brown sugar

1. Preheat the oven to 375° F. In the bowl of an electric mixer, combine the flour, sugar, baking powder and salt. Add the butter and milk and beat on medium speed for 2 minutes. Add the egg and vanilla and beat 2 minutes longer, scraping down the sides of the bowl. Set the batter aside.

2. Arrange the peaches in a circle over the bottom of a nonstick 8-inch round cake pan coated with vegetable cooking spray. Sprinkle the brown sugar evenly over the peaches. Pour the cake batter over the fruit.

3. Bake 30 to 35 minutes, or until a toothpick inserted in the center comes out clean. Cool in the pan 5 minutes, then turn out onto a cake platter or large plate. Let cool completely before serving.

Peach Bourbon Shortcakes

8 SERVINGS   14% CALORIES FROM FAT   207 CALORIES PER SERVING

1½ cups all-purpose flour
1 tablespoon baking powder
½ teaspoon salt
2 ounces low-fat cream cheese or Neufchâtel cheese
1 tablespoon butter, cut into small pieces
½ cup skim milk
4 medium peaches, peeled, seeded and thinly sliced, or 1 can (16 ounces) sliced peaches in light syrup, drained
¼ cup sugar
1 teaspoon cornstarch
¼ cup bourbon

1. Preheat the oven to 425° F. In a food processor, combine the flour, baking powder and salt. Pulse briefly to mix. Add the cream cheese and butter and process until the mixture resembles coarse meal. With the machine on, add the milk and mix just until the dough forms a ball around the blades.

2. Turn out the dough onto a lightly floured work surface and roll out into a ½-inch-thick circle. Use a 2-inch round cookie cutter to form 8 shortcakes. Arrange the shortcakes on a nonstick baking sheet and prick all over with a fork. Bake 10 to 12 minutes, or until lightly browned.

3. Meanwhile, in a medium saucepan, combine the peaches, sugar and cornstarch. Cook over medium heat, stirring often, until the peaches give up their juices and the liquid boils and thickens, about 3 minutes. Remove from the heat and stir in the bourbon.

4. Use a large serrated knife to split the shortcakes horizontally in half. Spoon about one-third of the peaches and sauce onto the bottoms of the shortcakes. Cover with the tops and spoon the remaining peaches over all. Serve at once.

Peaches Poached in Bourbon

4 Servings   30% Calories from fat   142 Calories per serving

¹/₂ cup sugar
¹/₂ cup bourbon
4 large peaches, peeled
¹/₃ cup heavy cream
¹/₄ teaspoon vanilla extract
1¹/₂ tablespoons chopped pecans

1. In a medium saucepan, combine the sugar and bourbon with 1 cup water. Bring to a boil over high heat. Add the peaches, reduce the heat to medium-high and poach, turning frequently, until tender, 10 to 12 minutes. Remove from the heat, transfer the peaches to a bowl and set aside.

2. Return the saucepan with the liquid to medium heat and boil rapidly until reduced by half, about 5 minutes. Pour the liquid over the peaches and let cool to room temperature. Cover and refrigerate 2 to 4 hours, or overnight, until chilled.

3. In a medium bowl, whip the cream with the vanilla until stiff. To serve, cut the chilled peaches in half and remove the pits. Place 2 peach halves in 4 dessert dishes. Top each with a spoonful of whipped cream and sprinkle the pecans on top.

Roasted Pears with Blackberries

The blackberries give the pears a beautiful color and an interesting, tart flavor. Because they are so seedy, though, I strain them after cooking, so only the tasty juices are served. For roasting, use pears that are firm but not rock hard.

4 Servings   13% Calories from fat   238 Calories per serving

4 medium pears, peeled, quartered and cored
1 cup blackberries
½ cup sugar
1 tablespoon butter, cut into small pieces

1. Preheat the oven to 425° F. Place the pears, blackberries and sugar in the bottom of an 8 × 11-inch baking dish. Toss gently to mix. Dot the butter over the top.

2. Bake, stirring once or twice, 20 to 25 minutes, until the pears are tender. With a slotted spoon, transfer the pears to a serving bowl.

3. Strain the berries and juices from the baking dish into a strainer set over a bowl, pressing down to extract as much juice as possible. Pour the blackberry juice over the pears and serve.

Watermelon Ice

6 SERVINGS   1% CALORIES FROM FAT   42 CALORIES PER SERVING

2 tablespoons sugar
2 teaspoons fresh lemon juice
3 cups watermelon pulp, seeded

1. In a small saucepan, combine the sugar and lemon juice with 2 tablespoons water. Cook over medium-high heat, stirring, until the sugar is dissolved, about 3 minutes. Set aside to cool.

2. In a food processor, combine the watermelon with the syrup. Puree until smooth. Transfer to an ice cream maker and freeze according to the manufacturer's instructions. (Alternatively, place in an 8 × 11-inch baking dish and freeze, stirring occasionally, until large crystals are formed, about 5 hours. Transfer to a food processor and blend until smooth.) Place in a covered container and freeze 1 hour longer, or until solid.

Meringue Plum Cake with Sherry

Similar to angel food cake, this confection is light, airy and balanced with an interesting mixture of plums and sherry. Use only the ripest fruit available and leave the skin on for color.

6 TO 8 SERVINGS   3% CALORIES FROM FAT   160 CALORIES PER SERVING

6 plums, pitted and quartered
½ cup dry sherry
½ cup plus 1 tablespoon sugar
3 egg whites
½ teaspoon cream of tartar
½ cup all-purpose flour
Vegetable cooking spray

1. In a small bowl, combine the plums, sherry and 1 tablespoon of the sugar. Stir well to blend, cover and let stand at room temperature 1 to 2 hours.

2. Combine the egg whites and the remaining ½ cup sugar in an electric mixer. Beat on high speed until stiff, about 2 minutes. Add the cream of tartar and beat 10 to 12 minutes longer, or until shiny and creamy. In 3 or 4 batches sift the flour over the egg whites and fold in with a rubber spatula.

3. Preheat the oven to 300° F. Coat an 8-inch round cake pan with vegetable cooking spray. Arrange the plums over the bottom of the pan. Fill with the meringue mixture. Bake 45 minutes, or until a toothpick inserted in the center of the cake comes out clean. Turn out to cool on a lightly oiled wire rack.

Carolina Summer Pudding

This is a variation on the old-fashioned English summer pudding. Neither contains any pudding. Don't let the simple ingredients fool you. This is a light and intensely flavored dessert with lots of character. Substitute currants, raspberries or mulberries, depending on which is at its seasonal best in the market or in the garden.

6 TO 8 SERVINGS   6% CALORIES FROM FAT   202 CALORIES PER SERVING

> *6 to 8 thin slices of thinly sliced, firm-textured white bread*
> *4 cups blackberries*
> *4 cups blueberries*
> *½ cup sugar*

1. Remove the crusts from the bread. Reserve 1 or 2 slices to cover the top of the pudding. In a 2-quart glass bowl, arrange the remaining slices to cover the bottom and sides of the bowl, trimming as necessary.

2. In a large nonreactive saucepan, combine the blackberries, blueberries, sugar and 1 tablespoon water. Bring to a simmer over moderate heat and cook, stirring often, until the berries give off their juices, about 2 minutes. Immediately pour into a heatproof bowl and cool to room temperature.

3. Pour the berries and all accumulated juices into the bread-lined mold. Cover the top with the reserved bread slices. Place a plate on top and weigh down with heavy cans, a paperweight, a brick or any similar object. Refrigerate overnight.

4. To serve, unmold the pudding onto a round platter just before serving. Cut into wedges with a large serrated knife.

Kentucky Mint Ice

This ice is shaved off the top with a spoon and used to garnish fresh berries, melon or chilled grapefruit and oranges. Add a spoonful to iced tea for a real Southern treat.

6 Servings   1% Calories from fat   41 Calories per serving

> *12 large sprigs of fresh mint*
> *¼ cup sugar*
> *Juice of 3 lemons (about ¾ cup)*

1. Place the mint in a 12-inch piece of cheesecloth and bring up the corners to meet in the middle. Tie securely with white kitchen string. Use the handle of a large knife or a rolling pin to pound the mint until it is mashed.

2. In a medium saucepan, combine the sugar with ½ cup of water. Cook over low heat, stirring occasionally, until the sugar is dissolved, about 1 minute. Remove from the heat and add 1½ cups of water and the lemon juice. Drop the bundle of mint into the syrup and let stand until cooled to room temperature.

3. Remove the mint and squeeze to let as much liquid as possible run back into the pan; discard the mint. Pour the syrup into an ice cream maker and freeze according to the manufacturer's instructions. (Alternatively, place in an 8 × 11-inch baking dish and freeze, stirring occasionally, until large crystals are formed, about 5 hours. Transfer to a food processor and blend until smooth.) Place in a covered container and freeze 1 hour longer, or until solid.

Index